Pasquale Verdicchio

DEVILS IN PARADISE

WRITINGS ON POST-EMIGRANT CULTURES

GUERNICA

Toronto/Buffalo/Lancaster

1997

Antonio D'Alfonso, editor.
Guernica Editions Inc.
P.O. Box 117, Station P, Toronto (Ontario), Canada M5S 2S6
250 Sonwil Drive, Buffalo, N.Y. U.S.A. 14225-5516
Gazelle, Falcon House, Queen Square, Lancaster LA1 1RN U.K.

The Publisher gratefully acknowledges the support of the Canada Council
of the Arts, The Ontario Arts Council, the Department of Canadian
Heritage (Multiculturalism), and the University of California Regents for
our publishing program.

Legal Deposit — Fourth Quarter
National Library of Canada
Library of Congress Card Number: 97-72387

Canadian Cataloguing in Publication data
Verdicchio, Pasquale, 1954-
Devils in paradise: writings on post-emigrant cultures
(Essay series ; 24)
Included bibliographical references.
ISBN 1-55071-027-3
1. Italian Canadians 2. Italian Americans. I Title. II. Series: Essay series
(Toronto, Ont.) ; 24.
E49.2.I8V47 1997 305.85'1071 C97-900503-5

Contents

The starting point of critical elaboration is the consciousness of what one really is and knowing one's self as a product of the historical process to date, which has deposited in you an infinity of traces, without leaving an inventory. It is therefore imperative at the outset to compile such an inventory.

Antonio Gramsci

Few people know
my whole
name.
Nor
if the name
they call me
is real.

Amiri Baraka

Subalterns Abroad

Italian Canadian Writing Between Nations and Cultures

Il vero divorzio è l'emigrazione.

Antonio D'Alfonso
The Other Shore

If emigration could have helped the working class to emancipate itself, it would never have existed.

Marco Micone
Voiceless People

Involuntary estrangement from one's place of birth is akin to existence under colonial circumstances and takes the place of colonialism as a conditioning force in contemporary history. If the result of emigration, and other such multifaceted terms of experience, is not an altogether negation of cultural expression, often it is the deferral of cultural enunciation for the émigré or colonized. In the case of the latter, we have "post-colonial" as the qualifying term of specificity and a critical body that continues to evolve in the exploration of post-colonial subjectivity, imperialist coordination of culture and its undoing. For emigration we have no such coinage. Perhaps, "postnationalism" might offer a starting point from which a critique could extend, and "emigration" (due to economics, politics, religion) would function as an explicit site of engagement under the heading of postnationalism.

Such parameters are readily applicable to the large portion of the Southern Italian population that was transplanted to the new social contexts of the U.S.A. and Canada as emigrants.[1] As history shows, these North American democracies were, and are, not as accepting of cultural diversity as might be given to believe.[2] Upon arrival to the shores of these nations, many groups have found it necessary to render their culture less visible to the world outside of their homes.[3] Through my analysis, I hope to make space for e/im-migrant culture as a variety of postcolonial expression for Southern Italians.

The need for cultural expression is hard to suppress, as is well illustrated by the amount of cultural production by minorities now finding a successful and eager market. Of course, such expression also represents a critique of the extant power structure that continues to limit diversity through prescriptions of national identity. In Canada, while many minority writers and artists have been at work for some time, their production began to find venues for exposure around the late 1970s and early 1980s. The first Italian Canadian anthology, *Roman Candles,* was published in 1978 by a small press and edited by poet Pier Giorgio Di Cicco who sought to come to terms with a background that had been partially buried and discarded. The following quotes from Di Cicco's preface are telling of a too common phenomenon that touches all minorities to some extent.

> In 1974 I returned to Italy for the first time in twenty-odd years. I went, biased against a legacy that had made growing up in North America a difficult but not impossible chore (or so I thought). I went out of curiosity, and came back to Canada conscious of the fact that I'd been a man without a country for most of my life. And I became bitter at the thought that most people carry on day after day deeply aware that they do so on the land upon which they were born. It became clear to me that they had something immediately and emotionally at stake with their environment. That phenomenon was something I had had to construct at every effort to feel relevant in an English country . . .

In searching for contributors, I found isolated gestures by isolated poets, isolated mainly by the condition of nationalism prevalent in Canada in the last ten years. However pluralistic the landscape seemed to be to sociologists, the sheer force of Canadianism had been enough to intimidate all but the older "unofficial language" writers . . . [The anthology] ranges from poems that directly speak from a displaced sensibility to poems that are not conscious of any such dilemma. All the poets included have one sure thing in common — they are not emigrants. They were brought here by their families at an early age, and three were born in North America. They are in the fortunate and tragic position of having to live with two cultures, one more exterior than the other. (9-10)

The sense of displacement expressed by Di Cicco is perhaps the common denominator to any writer working in a language other than the mother-tongue, within the context of another culture.

The problems associated with Italians in Canada and, most obviously, in the U.S.A., due to greater pressures and a longer time in which to assimilate, are in my opinion the result of a continuous repression of culture. The colonial conditions that denied cultural expression in Southern Italy before and after unification did not find an outlet in terms of what we today have come to call "postcolonial discourse." Unification of the peninsula in 1861 did not in fact liberate the South; it merely altered the colonial structure. Southern Italian culture has generally subsisted as a colonial culture, and much of that cultural production falls into a category that escapes the particularity of the group that produces it in order to find a function at the service of the "nation." An example of this would be found in Benedetto Croce's position as an intellectual, as proposed by Gramsci.[4] Croce's great service to the Italian nation and its culture was his disservice to the South through his facilitation of the absorption of Southern radical intellectuals into a national bourgeoisie, thereby denying the possibility of a Southern revolution.[5]

The numbers of colonized subjects that left their land for elsewhere and the conditions that received them abroad were such that cultural subordination became an almost voluntary act dictated by survival. The recent expressions of Italian identity in the U.S.A. and Canada must be recognized as expressions of postcolonial discourse for Southern Italians. This presents an interesting phenomenon that alters not only the relationship of Italians to their adopted countries, but invariably tends toward a change in the entrenched view of Southern Italians specifically and Italian emigrants in general in Italian culture.

The emigration of millions of Italians, two thirds of them from southern regions of Italy, evolved from specific sociopolitical and economic parameters. For this reason, I find it most proper to consider the question of Italian Canadian writing through the works of a writer equally concerned with the region known in Italy as "the South and Islands."[6]

In his meditations on "the Southern question" and "the role of intellectuals," among other subjects, Antonio Gramsci, the Sardinian founder of the Italian Communist Party, provides approaches to questions of cultural determinacy that are valid in a contemporary context. How does the work of Gramsci help us today to understand the relationship of a group, such as that formed by Italian Canadian writers, to official culture(s)? How will understanding such relationships help us to better identify the overwhelming "official" mechanisms at work in the maintenance of a system of dominance and subordination? These are some of the questions I wish to explore through a Gramscian lens aimed at a fragment of that emigrant population so central to much of his writing.

The makeup of a writers' groups such as the Association of Italian Canadian Writers is quite varied. Though the Association is not solely represented by southerners, they certainly form the majority of the group. Some of the writers were born in Italy, others not; most however are the offspring of parents who did not have the possibility or the occasion to pursue a formal education. Their background is proletarian or subproletarian, either of urban or rural extraction. The languages they speak differ from one another and most are far from the standardized Italian taught in schools. As a result their participation in the governing of their land of origin and the structuring of its official culture has been at best marginal. These women and men come from historically inactive or hidden groups whose potential to achieve the cohesiveness of an historical bloc and thus make its presence felt was further truncated by emigration from economic and/or socio-political oppression.[7]

The Association of Italian Canadian Writers meets with some regularity and sponsors readings and talks, all of which provides a sense of community and communication for writers who had been working alone along the margins of what may be termed "official" Canadian culture (which is in itself a problematic designation). It is fairly common to now describe this type of relationship to "official" culture as "minor," a term borrowed from Deleuze and Guattari's essay, *Kafka* (Deleuze, 16-17).

With respect to our concerns, the elements of "minor literature" are as follows:

- "The deterritorialization of language" involves an extended series of languages: dialect, standardized tongue, Canadian English vs. American English (and the relationship of both to British English), and the relationship of Quebecois French to Parisian French;
- The "political immediacy" of minority expression calls for and requires the achievement of a critical stance regarding the immigrant condition;
- The "collective assemblage of enunciation" relates, in our case, to the existence of the Association of Italian Canadian Writers itself (though so far only in a weak and

uncoordinated manner). In their self-recognition and organization into the Association (1986), Italian Canadian writers are potentially representative of a "historical bloc."

Anne Showstack Sassoon, in her discussion of the concept of "historical bloc" in *Gramsci's Politics* (1980), regards the historical bloc as being "specific to the national context," and suggests that, while there is an "international conjuncture, a special emphasis is placed on the national dimension as the basic unit to be analyzed" (121). It could be argued, however, that while the emergence of an historical bloc may be forever stalled within a particular national situation, within another it may indeed flourish. The self-representation of countries like Canada as "multicultural mosaics" provides, at least on the surface, the possibility of forming an historical bloc for immigrant populations.[8]

The "international conjuncture" quoted by Sassoon is of course the end to which Marxism aspires, but it is an insufficient vantage point for isolated, unrepresented groups whose international internal references may be overlooked. For example, the study of Italian Canadian, Chinese Canadian, or Haitian Canadian writing purely as a Canadian phenomenon, identified only with the plight of either the Canadian working or immigrant class, would be both incomplete and misleading, as would be a reading that merely reduced their relationships to a static dominant/subordinate dichotomy on the cultural level.

To unpack and breathe life into this relationship, terms such as "hegemony" must be reviewed in a renewed light. Again, I must stress the applicability of Gramsci on the topic at hand even though his concepts were primarily based in a very particular Italian context. The linguistic source/reality of such concepts is of specific importance, given the relationship of Italy's South and Islands to the rest of the country.

In his *Prison Notebooks* (1987), Antonio Gramsci makes use of the term hegemony to express the domination of one class or group over others, yet I feel that the complexity of his discussion is less definitive and simplifistic. As the *Notebooks* reveal, hegemony cannot in itself signify domination. In order for the concept of hegemony to take on a sense of domination it must be backed by a coercive political apparatus, at which time it ceases to be hegemony and becomes the State. A plurality of hegemonies may coexist within what Gramsci termed an "expansive hegemony." This designation is discussed by Chantall Mouffe in her essay "Hegemony and New Political Subjects: Toward a New Concept of Democracy," whose reconsideration of the influence of hegemonic theory is part of her co-operative work with Ernesto Laclau. The association of the term with what Mouffe defines as the achievement of "plural democracy" reasserts Gramsci's use of "expansive hegemony" to express an ever active interplay of cultural entities in the creation of culture, not necessarily culminating in the emergence of a dominant group.[9]

Beginning with the assumption that subalternity and marginality are expressed through linguistic manipulations, as well as explicit thematics, Italian writing abroad needs to be recognized as one that presents variations not only in the dominant/subordinate dichotomy, as expressed in Italy in the North/South relationship and the history of emigration, but also as this dichotomy plays itself out in North American contexts.

The expressions of cultural identity that have emerged under the labels of Italian American and Italian Canadian are indicative of different assimilationist policies. Canada, with its complexity of a double (English/French), if unbalanced, center toward which other cultural expressions must articulate themselves, actually hides a stalled hegemonic interplay under its varied surface. One would think that in Quebec, if only because of the Quebecois' own struggle for cultural survival within an ineffectual dominant/subordinate system, a process of "expansive hegemony" might be at work.

However, Quebec manifests a constant reassertive strategy in its relation to minority groups, that is, a strategy of containment by which linguistic and educational laws designate a minority's mode of expression. This failure to extend to others the rights of cultural presence that Quebecois (mostly, but not singularly, with French descendants) declare for themselves is a serious problem that maintains the system in a static tension. Such attitudes eventually meet with forceful assertions of cultural identity by other groups, and recent incidents concerning not only the Mohawk but other native groups are a result of this sort of blindness on the part of Quebecois.

The 1970s were an instance of this type of tension as experienced and acted upon by Canada's "other" official population; future tensions may be a direct result of a set of circumstances which perpetuate a system similar to what the Quebecois fear in their relationship to so-called English Canada. The Quebecois struggle for recognition prepared the right set of circumstances for other groups to take up similar causes. Yet Quebec's need to ensure its survival has resulted in a state coercive apparatus not dissimilar to that of English Canada. These systems only barely hold on to their "hegemonic principle" of culture and will in time have to resort to other (violent?) means to maintain their dominance. Ironically, it would seem that the reason why Canadian society constantly fails to come together as a bipolar English/French representation is directly tied to the possibilities that the recognition of Quebec as an autonomous cultural society provides.

Here, and this could refer to Canada, the U.S.A., Germany, or to whichever place Italians may have migrated, our culture is known only in its singular, concentrated space: for example, the Italian community or Italian culture as perceived by non-Italians. In Italy, maybe not surprisingly, cultural diversity is still a point of incredible conflict.[10] But, whether internal, to Milano or Torino, or external, to Germany or Canada, the disorientation these hegemonic fragments of immigrants experienced has come to stand as a mode of cultural opposition wherever they have settled. As with all émigré or refugee groups, the nature of the distancing from their community represents a deprivation of a sense of historical continuity. Their experience is largely undocumented or disregarded in their places of origin; and in their new land they are further discontinuous, since no history precedes them.

Italian Canadians are suspended between the English/French Canadian reality and their own cultural background, the result of which one could imagine as a center/margin relationship in which, every day, every single act and thought enacts a continual switching of positions from the center to the margins, and back again. There is a play of multiple personalities and unstable subject positions where the languages of thought and expression do not necessarily match, where intellectual and social life conflict, and where the political opposition to a dominant culture often manifests itself as an internal, rather than external, experience.

Italian Canadian writing represents a site of reterritorialization tending toward the formation of a historical bloc, even if the writers share only a partial history and their linguistic histories are dissimilar in their initial deterritorialization. Within this context, Italy is an abstraction that cannot be given dominion, just as the English language cannot. Multiculturalism proposes a structure for mystification by which people become the creation of the cultural rather than vice versa. Multiculturalism, or institutionalized ethnicism, dictates the parameters for de/re-territorialization, and neutralizes the potentially antagonistic "political immediacy and [the] collective assemblage of enunciation" of any cultural agent.

Today, the languages of colonialism are themselves being colonized by the very elements they once sought to subdue. The writers who have taken the colonialists' language as a means of expressing their own culture are many: Nigeria's Chinua Achebe, Nuruddin Farah of Somalia, and Shiva Naipaul are among them. Nations that find themselves overwhelmed by the influx of diverse populations are hard pressed to define a national characteristic that, in turn, would represent their relationship with the rest of the world. It has become common that, having reached a certain point in their development, nations have had to give recognition (albeit limited) to the variety of voices that inhabit them. To quote Giovanni Arrighi: "Whenever the political claim (and/or definition by others) is less than that of state sovereignty, we tend to call this group an 'ethnic group,' whatever the basis of the claim, be it common language, common religion, common skin color, or fictive common ancestry" (25).

Ethnic is thus a subset of the minor condition described above, or a condition necessary to it, thereby also representative of a threat to the dominant. In order to neutralize the expression of the ethnic, in other words to return it to the status described by Arrighi, it has been necessary for official cultures to institutionalize the term, and "circumscribe it by time," as another cultural "-ism" — ethnicism.

Canada's "Multicultural Mosaic" is a euphemism for institutionalized multiculturalism, which is, in turn, a "strategy of containment" adopted out of necessity by the dominant culture in order to maintain its power identity. As it becomes obvious by what is published and what is not, whether and where it is anthologized, and whether any attention is paid to it in general, or whether it is funded by one agency or another, the "strategy of containment" involves a choice by which only a selected (non-representative) sample is allowed to speak for/from a particular ethnic group. The end result, of course, is one of ethnicism or culturalism, in other words an external imposition of identity that denies past and present history in favor of abstractions such as nationhood and nationality.

Among such abstractions we must include "ethnicism," "multiculturalism" and the "Italian" and "Canadian" nationalities (in their singular and hyphenated forms). All of these are ideological categories not only because they represent strategies of containment in the definition of meaning, but because they suppress alternative meanings that are a basic requirement in the interplay or challenges of hegemony.

The work read, presented, critiqued, and discovered at Association of Italian Canadian Writers meetings is often relegated, by the official culture, to a sphere that, while inextricably connected to others such as the social, the political, the historical, is approached as if it were divorced from all these. When lip-service is given an "ethnic" culture, it is done as if that culture had developed *tabula rasa* and in isolation. Immigrant, ethnic, minor, marginal cultures are products of definite socio-historical conditions that, whether originating abroad or within a single national setting, represent a suppressed element in the hegemonic dialectic.

With the acquisition of a language of expression, with the opening provided by language as an antagonistic tool, Italian Canadian writers have been able to turn the English language back toward those who call it their mother tongue. By stressing latinate vocabulary, by the insertion of Italian syntactical forms, and by the inclusion of linguistic elements that represent the utterances of immigrant culture, these writers have altered the semantic field of English, thereby denying expected meaning. The expression of Italian Canadian "silence" becomes Anglo Canada's interpretative silence.[11] Here begins a genealogy that provides its subject with a position that stands in opposition to a given history.

The re-instatement of a subject in history necessitates a recognition of the subject's historical situation, which must take place at the level of aggregate subject.[12] This would also be reflective of the forces that act upon it; becoming conscious of the conditions that outline the subject, one discovers its potential for antagonism. I would like it to be clear that this is not a call for community. The heterogeneity of the Italian Canadian group would negate any such attempt. Rather, it is a proposal for the exploration of an historical commonality that does not erase the group's cultural diversity but reinforces it.

In her essay "Contemporary Italo-Canadian Literature," Susan Iannucci states that "Italo-Canadian writing is circumscribed by time. It is the product of a moment in a writer's life, and that moment vanishes . . . Italy filters through in past tense; their present is Canadian" (Perin, 225-226). Such a questionable conclusion is strongly based on the belief that "ethnicity" or cultural identity is something discernible in themes and subject matter, and that once explicit treatment of certain themes becomes invisible they have been surpassed or overcome. This attitude supports the formation of institutionalized multiculturalism agencies which require a specific set of themes of a writer in order to be qualified as "ethnic." A failure to conform to prescribed ethnic formulas leaves some writers marginalized to an even greater degree, due to their double exclusion from both the "official" and "ethnic" categories.

What makes it possible to describe Italian Canadian writing, and by extension any hyphenated writing, as "the product of a moment," is buried deep in the blindness of the historical causes and effects of emigration. It is fair to say that while emigrants physically leave behind family, friends, and home they also leave behind a cultural past. What is more important is that such a cultural past may often have been deemed secondary to the official culture of their land, or have even remained unexpressed due to oppressive pressure of national compromise.

Immigrants, upon arrival in their new home, are faced with another choice which, more often than not, dictates that they must once again suppress their own culture in order to embrace that of their host country.

And so, while the writing of Italian Canadians may be "the product of a moment in a writer's life," I would oppose

Iannucci's "moment" with Marshall McLuhan's "moment of change." At the moment of expression of particularity, a work defines a border with other works and comes to transform its expression into a moment of challenge rather than a short-lived instance.[13] Iannucci's view fails the very group it is analyzing by regarding that moment merely as a stage resulting from the meeting of Canadian culture and perceiving it, not as another culture but, as a lack within one's own culture.

The supposed resolution of the crisis is achieved through a realization that leads to finding one's "Canadian" identity, as ambiguous as that may be. This approach, even while making weak overtures to heterogeneity, blatantly valorizes one culture over another, and disregards the influences at work in a phenomenon such as e/im-migration. Further, it facilitates and propagates the image of an ethnic literature as nothing more than nostalgic portrayals of the possibility or impossibility of a return to an illusionary rootedness. Often this work can be deeply reactionary, and may in fact further alienate the subject not only from its new situation but also from the distant and changing one it has left behind.

Alternative reactions to displacement may come to light either as rejuvenated hegemonic representations, by which the writing subject engages the new culture in a critical dialogue that includes an awareness of his or her own historical situation, or as an attempt at full integration into, and denial of difference from, the official culture of arrival. Whatever the expression, it results from a contradictory construction of the subject, and an attempt to answer that contradiction. I believe that the most interesting expression of the Italian Canadian as expatriates comes from the instigation of cultural dialogue, and from the antagonism that it represents for the official culture. Writers such as Antonio D'Alfonso, Marco Micone, and Dôre Michelut seek to shake culture at its linguistic roots, an act which (in the spirit of the Vichian verum factum) opens the possibility of knowledge to those who undertake the challenge of making a language new to suit their expression.

In *The Other Shore* (1986), Antonio D'Alfonso closes the book with a section entitled "Il nuovo barocco," in which he states:

> I shall no longer write (in English). This notebook in which I move ahead. Alone. A step forward. A stop towards the ultimate horizon, the only path. To find myself. Ourselves. A step backwards . . . The "moment of change": when one becomes another. The exact moment of transformation. The action fixed, the verb metamorphosing into a noun. The action and the verb possess a morality of their own, which rises from within; whereas the Baroque freeze frame — the artistic noun — known nothing of morality . . . It exists per se and appears before our eyes naked, without pessimism or optimism, as it it were created by a mathematical force beyond our control. (155-156)

D'Alfonso's "I shall no longer write (in English)" marks the instatement of silence and antagonism toward English Canada. However, rather than choose one of the other languages at his disposal (Italian or French), he continues to write in English. What begins as a contestation of English, bi-lingual Canada's dominant language, takes on the appearance of an act of antagonism toward Quebec and Italy as well. Indeed, the contestation retains its multidirectionality and should rather be taken as the assertion of having acquired the language of expression of Canada's "dominant" culture in order to unveil its silent dimension and thereby subvert its power position. Those who believe that D'Alfonso "shall no longer write" and therefore stop reading, will not hear the emerging voice and will not notice the "moment of change" in which their language (English) "becomes another['s]."

Silence is also the currency of Dôre Michelut's poetics. In *Loyalty to the Hunt* (1986), silence is expressed neither through Italian nor English, but through the use of Friulano.

This is a silent language in many respects, first because it is an oral language and, most importantly, because it is ranked in a subordinate position (as a dialect) to Italian. The piece entitled "Ne storie" (36) reflects the paradox of orality, where reference is made to language but language is often superfluous to voice. There can be no answer to the (written) question "Dulà sêtu stade fin cumò?" ("Where have you been?"), for originally Friulano had no written language and therefore its written form can only be a fiction. What the reader receives is a voice that, since it affords no linguistic reference, may well be overlooked. Despite this, Michelut writes in Friulano, a language the use of which brings on feelings such as "bitterness that seeps into my mouth, that shocks my teeth like icy well water" (37).

Rather than a sensation that would keep one from using the language though, Michelut's "bitterness" reveals itself to be a viable contestatory element in opposition to written language and the fixation of meaning. The memory of its orality is what enables one to "see," in other words, to hear and to understand: "And we see each other only when the Stèle floods from the mouth of the storyteller who once upon a time would go from barn to barn and say . . . " (37). While the author does provide English translations to her compositions, I would suggest that they represent a silencing gesture to prevent any English reader from asserting authority over the text's inherent absence. Michelut bypasses both Italian language and an English representation of herself, and gives center stage to the emerging Friulan voice.

While the preceding examples are of a silence imposed on the English reader, in the case of Marco Micone's plays the silencing is a result of language interference, not unusual within immigrant family groups. Micone's *Voiceless People* (1984) is one example of the problems in cultural adaptation that are the result of generational differences. The attempts at acculturation that lead to conflict among family members are also the cause of internalized frustration and the cessation of communication. The playwright's more recent *Babele* is extremely effective for its polyphonic structure, the white noise and silence that hinders communication, within a family whose members have adopted different languages of expression and can no longer find a common ground.[14] In the following excerpt Pasquale, the father, proudly boasts about his son Tony's ability to speak "English like an Englishman and French better than the French." This he reports in his own dialect to a Quebecois visitor who does not understand the language; nevertheless, while boasting about his son's linguistic capabilities he complains that Tony has forgotten Italian:

> Pasquale (*A Jacques, rapidamente dimostrando fierezza*): Ha visc'te come parle 'nglese. Pare ca 'nce vo fa'. Però . . . Parle 'nglese come nu 'Nglese e u francese meglie di Francese. I' u sacce, p' cchè a isse u capische, mentre i Francese d' qua manche na parole. (*Poi, come se gli rivelasse un segreto.*) Sule u taliane, nu parle tante boune. (*Riprende il tono normale.*) Quille, doppe, u pov're uagliò, già 'nze ni tè da parlà. Doppe a vute a sf'rtune da capità miezz'a nuie. (*Più forte in ottimo italiano.*) Abbiamo dimenticato finanche l'italiano. (*Poi continua in dialetto.*) A ch' serv'ne i solde, i case, i mach'ne e tant'atra rrobbe, simme perze a cosa cchiù bella ch' c' sta. N'n sapimme cchiù bella ch' c' sta. N'n sapimme cchiù parla. (*Con rabbia contenuta.*) Di vote, v' nnesse tutte e m' n' iesse . . . (*Dirigendosi verso gli spettatori.*) Che v'fa, a vuie, quande u figlie vuosc'tre v' parle 'nglese o francese sapenne ca vuie capite sule u mulisane o u bruzzese? [15]

While these three examples briefly go to show the great variety of work produced within the Italian Canadian group, their salient feature is in their position of contradiction and antagonism. This places them, through language, at the center of the mechanisms of cultural production. The work of these authors is a response to the external forces that have constructed their subjectivity as immigrants, and represents an attempt to unveil those same forces. Micone and D'Alfonso's epigrams, quoted at the outset of this essay, demonstrate that the antagonism is not only addressed at Canada's construction of their subjectivity but also at Italy's. This declares the immigrant's autonomy from both influences and clears a ground for further cultural activity that speaks of itself and is not merely the mirror of another's image.

In current debates on subaltern cultures, it has been acceptable to consider the position of subaltern groups solely within the context of their present national situation.[16] This designation, however, is not universally applicable, given the fact that many such groups have definite ties to other official cultures and traditions external to that of their immediate residency. Whatever the forces of their decontextualization, be they economic, political, or other, these groups maintain a historical and cultural link with their places of provenance.

Cultural interplay is directly related to language and the undertaking of an historical critique through linguistic means. Such an exercise leads to the consciousness of the "moment of change" quoted by Antonio D'Alfonso in his discussion of the "New Baroque." This designation that he would apply to expressions such as Italian Canadian writing, and for which I am indebted to D'Alfonso, is from Marshall McLuhan's discussion of the Baroque: "Baroque art and poetry sought to unify disparate facets and experiences by directing attention to the moment of change" (McLuhan, 17-18). The quotation's source is of added significance, given McLuhan's concept of "global village" and the cultural interrelatedness it describes. Placed in the context of minor literature, this brings us back to the moment of challenge, the point where cultures touch and mingle, where they define their positions; the moment that both unifies and distances the populations of a land.

Italian Canadian writers must assess their value within the moments of "departure" and "arrival" that cannot but al-

ter those who undertake the journeys, as well as their hosts
and originators, thereby representing a criticism both of the
place left and of the place reached. Yet these moments must
find articulation in order to be of value. Such articulations are
to be found in the work of D'Alfonso, Michelut, and Micone,
through their use of language, and in particular in their use of
metaphor, and the instrumentation of silence and deferment
of meaning. They, and other Italian Canadian writers, use the
inheritance of silence against itself in their cultural self-
assertion, establishing its function not only through metaphor
but as a metaphor in itself.

M.J. Michael Fisher, in "Ethnicity and the Post-Modern
Arts of Memory" (Clifford, 194-233), comments that "the
search for a sense of ethnic identity is a (re-)invention and discovery of a vision, both ethical and future-oriented. Whereas
the search for coherence is grounded in a connection to the
past, the meaning abstracted from that past, an important cri-
terion of coherence, is an ethic workable for the future" (196).
Fisher further says that "ethnicity is a process of inter-
references between two or more cultural traditions" (201).
This assignation of ambivalence to the "moment" finds con-
gruency with Gramsci, in his stressing of the importance of relationships within all of his concepts. Fisher's conclusions,
while not over-valuing either past or future, further make it
clear that the processes of cultural expression and "ethnic"
self-representation cannot be viewed as singular, unidirectional, and definitive.

Italian Canadian writers seem to be expressing a period
of conscientization that achieves something that may have remained unattainable in the Italian national context.[17] Among
them we find a flourishing of "organic intellectuals" who are
very specific in the expression of their immigrant position.
And, as immigration also supposes emigration, the moment of
challenge by these intellectuals is directed toward a critique of
both Italian and Canadian national policies of culture and
identity. In order not to digress on a discussion of the "organic

intellectual," it will suffice here to bridge this term with the "historical bloc" designation mentioned above. Briefly, Gramsci's "organic intellectual" is to be distinguished from the "traditional intellectual" in that she or he is the product of a particular group and upholds that group's cultural and political interests.[27] The line between the two types of intellectuals is a fine one, given that the acquired languages of communication for many, either English or French, are also the "official" languages. What differs from one group to another is the application and the mode of dissemination of that language. Of primary importance is the "organic intellectual's" responsibility to her or his constituency rather than to any other external institution.[18] In this context, Pier Giorgio Di Cicco's statement that for him the question is "not how does my viewpoint differ? but how am I differently seen in the view of the mainstream culture?" (*Transition*, 23) is all important, for it declares the automatic legitimacy of a culture that the dominant is constantly attempting to de-legitimate.

Di Cicco's statement opposes the point of view of many who find it hard to conceive of ethnic or immigrant writing removed from the influence of the dominant culture, and overlook the ties with the problems associated with Italian nationhood that are part and parcel of the condition. While much of this is unintended, it is nevertheless expressed, and has often worked its magic into the writings of Italian Canadian critics. In Joseph Pivato's essay "Nothing Left to Say: Italian-Canadian Writers," the distance that has insinuated itself between many em/im-migrants and the history of immigration is apparent:

> There is no recognized tradition of ethnic writing in Canada. We have had many writers in the unofficial languages but they have remained underground, invisible. For the majority culture, writers like Stephan Stephansson do not exist. There is no tradition of Italian-Canadian writing to which writers can belong

or against which they can react. Without a tradition
writers do not exist because they are writing in a vac-
uum . . . [The] dialectic with an established tradition is
not yet possible for Italian-Canadian writers, unless
they simply accept the still new English-language or
French-language situations. (*Transition,* 33)

Is Italian Canadian writing, or any ethnic writing, the expression of a moment which may indeed, as the title of Pivato's essay ironically suggests, leave these writers with nothing left to
say? No, because it is a result of historical events through
which immigrant writing persists, evolves, and makes itself felt
in the society at large.

The culture of "ethnic" writers, while a product of the
cultures of those who form the immigrant groups, cannot
claim to represent those same groups. To present the AICW as
the cultural representative of the "Italian community" in Canada would be nothing more than a variation upon the rule of
state, and accede to the perceived necessity to declare and
identify one's self with Canadian society's dominant dimension. While we are indeed partaking in the construction of a
new culture we cannot pretend to know what that culture may
be. Any agent describing hegemonic circulation must remain
distant from determinative temptations, lest she or he participate in the suffocation and atrophy of its expression.

In its own time, situated thought such as Gramsci's was
to a large extent denied the possibility of expression that is
now being exercised by groups such as the Italian Canadians.
And, if for Gramsci POSSIBILITY=FREEDOM, then the literary
production of Italian Canadians has introduced a range of possibilities into English which is potentially freeing for all users
of the language. Their work, and that of other cultural groups
within the Canadian context, goes to facilitate the dialectic between determinism and freedom by which a truly multicultural society may emerge.

The Borders of Writing

Nation, Language, Migration

What is the place of literature in the context of national culture? The examples of literature in the service of national identity, in which politics, ideology, philosophy, real or imagined citizenship and poetics intersect are many. Dante Alighieri, Jose Martí and Ernesto Cardenal are but a few of the names that come to mind in this context. Alternatively, in *Resistance Literature* (1987) Barbara Harlow analyzes various situations in which writing, and in particular poetry, is to be counted among the most effective modes of cultural resistance. Without detracting from the value of this proposition, I would like to suggest that perhaps it is also within such a definition that the contradictions of literary discourse and practice may be located.

While we may concur that poetry is "a force for mobilizing a collective response to occupation and domination and . . . a repository for popular memory and consciousness" (34), things come to a problematic head when this is coupled with the notion that "the role of poetry is . . . a major one . . . because it sustains, within the popular memory, national continuity" (34). The suggestion is that even when culture is used as a term of liberation against external forces of "occupation and domination," it nevertheless reproduces struggles and movements toward the designation of national identity or "national continuity."

With this in mind, I would like to touch upon the terms of my subtitle (Language, Nation, and Migration) in a roundabout manner so as to be able to link diverse trajectories in literary production. The influence of migration on the socio-economic development of the contemporary world has altered notions of "national continuity" through the insertion of non-nationals into apparently culturally homogeneous national systems. In fact, if there is any continuity it is to be searched for within the continuous deflection of a homogeneous culture rather than in its assertion. As such, questions regarding the continuity or discontinuity established by Chinese North American, Italian North American, Indian North American, and other immigrant groups in relation to a national situation must be analyzed. One must also take into consideration divergent nationalist discourses (within nation states) represented by the Native American version of nationalism as well as the various versions of Black nationalism. I will by no means touch on all of these issues here, but I do intend to trace lines of cultural intersection as they concern Italian North American literature, aspects of which may be applicable to parallel situations.

An important aspect of the Italian situation is the age old *questione della lingua* (the language problem). Given the linguistic diversity on the Italian peninsula, this question is as alive today as it was when Dante first approached it in the *De vulgari eloquentia*. Subsequently, *la questione della lingua* has been at the center of all intellectual debates on the "national" culture. The work of Alessandro Manzoni, for example, is representative of attempts at constructing a national language through literature. While these historical approaches are related to the emergence of the Italian nation, they lead us to similar concerns in contemporary Italian society. In attempting to assess the value of some sort of continuity or tradition, in other words to define a canon for Italian North American literature, I believe that the language question should be regarded as one of the most important conditioning elements, whether individuals work in Italian, in one of the so-called dialects, English, or French.

Part of the tradition that Italian North American writers can look to is that of Italian writers who challenge linguistic standardization within Italy. These writers offer tentative terms of comparison for Italian North American writers' concerns with language. I have therefore chosen to concentrate on a reading of Italian writers involved in linguistic "experimentation" alongside Italian North American writers involved in similar activities. While obviously not identical, the writers' strategies nevertheless converge in their poetic research and in their critique of cultural nationalism. By devising links among the writers considered herein I do not mean to insinuate the existence of an Italian immigrant "form" but merely suggest that there are forms related to the tendencies of resistance and non-official expression in Italy that may be of value to expatriate Italians. Concurrently, these suggestions are intended to be a partial reply to various claims that Italian North American writing is an expression without precedent tradition and/or merely a phase that will eventually extinguish itself. Such an opinion is supported by those who consider that the most valuable Italian expatriate writing is being produced by a stratum of "post-1968" intellectuals migrated to North America, most of whom are professors within Italian departments. This group usually writes in Italian and has always insisted on its Italian identity rather that identify as "immigrant Italian." By repeating official distinctions based on class categorizations to define who is or is not an immigrant, this group re-enforces negative stereotypes of Italian immigrants and presents itself as the only viable and valuable source of Italian culture abroad. This of course effectively discounts the value of much of Italian North American writing in English and other languages. All these arguments necessarily call into question considerations of canon and canon construction, which in my view cannot be divorced from the greater context of Italian literature and culture.

The determining aspect in the work of the writers I will present herein is that they activate poetics oppositional to prescribed categories of national identity such as institutionalized multiculturalism, official language policies, and the like. Italian North American writing, as that of other hyphenated groups, offers new dimensions to the critique of nation by overlaying strata of dialogue as it relates to other official and non-official literatures and, beyond that, in the interaction of English and French with Italian and its dialects.

The first writer I would like to propose in this comparative constitution is Emilio Villa. Born in Milano in 1914, Villa is one of the first post-futurist exponents of the experimental tendencies that would later be emulated by participants in various avant-garde movements, among them the Gruppo 63.[1] Representative of a radical position that mistrusts any and all languages for their potential to centralize and constrict culture. Villa applies continuous linguistic shifts that go from Italian to French to English to Latin and Greek and include mixtures and alterations of them.

Villa's distance from Italian culture grows beyond the linguistic level when, for a period in the early 1950s, he transfers to Brazil. His contact with the Noigandres group brought Villa back into contact with the works of Pound, Joyce, and cummings (Villa, 9). However, already in 1937, Villa had objected to Eliot and Pound's "poetics of vision" as too limiting and, returning to Dante who had influenced both American poets, he wrote: "non solo il 'visibile parlare' ma anche 'vision ch'a me si spiega' " (Villa, 10). The 'vision ch'a me si spiega' expresses the move in Villa's work toward the unfolding *(spiegarsi)* of empty space as a significant semantic component. By displacing words from their central position on the page and allowing the encroachment of space, Villa increases the dimensions of "silence" inherent in the written word. The problematic relationship between signifier and signified is exalted as linguistic signs begin to form associations beyond the norm at both the phonetic and semantic levels.

Villa's search for an agrammatical phoneme distant from the legislating logos is not toward a point of revelation and comprehension or recognition, but rather toward what Aldo Tagliaferri has termed "a pathos of distance and infinite metonymy" (Villa, 55). Villa's eventual abandonment of Italian for French, Latin, and Greek constitutes an attempt to totally distance himself from Italian literary institutions and his own "historic origins."

Villa's distancing from the Italian "logos" is also an attempt to approximate a more ideally heterogeneous Italian culture. The agglomeration of languages acquires a choric function that accompanies or glosses the silence that emerges from the tension produced by their juxtaposition. Sections 11 & 13 of *Seventeen Variations* represent instances in which the linguistic tension and the ideological stance of the work peers through, and readers are given a sampling of "purely phonetic" silence. The *questione della lingua* has for Emilio Villa implications quite different from the usual ones. For Villa the choice is not between a standardized language (Italian) and regional linguistic systems (dialects), but rather a choice involving any language that can oppose centralization.

As the multilingual context distances both poet and text from a concept of original language, their co-existence creates a new environment in which their reading leaves behind it a jet-stream of empty passage that resolves itself as the silent utterance of the past. Each linguistic turn alters the writer's (and reader's) relationship with the world and installs an infinite moment of reassessment and initiation. The tongue of initiation is the silence whose presence extends throughout the text in a multiple fashion as beginning or an end, and as a mediating vehicle of phonetic expression.

Andrea Zanzotto (1921) has stated that in his first books he "actually cancelled human presence, out of a form of distaste caused by historical events. [He] wanted only to speak of landscape, to return to a nature in which man had not been active. It was a psychological reflex-re-action to the devastation of war." This is certainly true of *Dietro il paesaggio* (Behind the Landscape) (1951), the first book to introduce this singular poet to an Italian scene at that time strongly under the influence of Neorealism.

If it is at all possible to generalize Zanzotto's poetics as a whole, it could be said to be a poetry centered around the rapport of the various linguistic possibilities open to a human biological/existential presence. Of course, such a work is directly tied to the historical presence and function of poetic language and form. Zanzotto's reconsideration of traditional language and forms (in works such as *Elegy and Other Verses,* 1954; IX *Eclogues, 1962; Galateo,* 1978, in which the presence of Tasso, Petrarca, Della Casa, and others looms large) seek to extend and test the limits of convention.

Zanzotto's modus operandi has been to trace his way back to elemental linguistic units via accepted or standardized linguistic expression. He achieves his goals by using alternative languages, like baby-talk and the dialect of the Veneto region where he lives. Zanzotto's "I," the writing subject, is rescued from its designation as pronoun and is established in the landscape as a noun, as opposed to I Novissimi 's attempts at erasing its presence altogether.

Fosfeni (1983) is one of Zanzotto's most complex collections in its exploration of the movement from topos to logos and their interaction. The following diagram

auto<—>bio<—>graphy

offered by Zanzotto in a piece written just before the publication of *Fosfeni,* expresses the movement of language in the poetic process, making the biological body the point of intersection. "Last Suppers," which opens the collection, presents a repeating finality that points to a continuous renewal of discursive tendencies. The Platonic or Biblical banquet multiplied ad infinitum offers an open ended poetic dialogue and the provisions that fuel that exercise.

Zanzotto refers to poetry as a "revomiting," which may remind us of Charles Olson's remark that "diet precedes language." This establishes a concept of language as a material that after ingestion and a close association with the body is ejected as a varied assortment of graphemes, phrases, letters, and verses. The final product is a gelatinous substance (present in the pages of Fosfeni as gel, ice, and the like) which aids in the "gelling" process of topos and logos. As this material leaves the body, it rejoins and alters the landscape as a climatic by-product (snow, ice, or frost). The resulting accumulation and coating is a consistent and coherent poetics upon which the poet treads. Associations are removed from geographically described limits of nation and language, and can be then contextualized within more generic and transnational scopes (landscapes and metereology).

I believe that it is in Villa's silent tensions and Zanzotto's wintry linguistic regurgitations that we find a significant point of reference for Italian Canadian writers. In a recent review of work by two Italian Canadian writers in the journal *Canadian Literature,* Lesley Clement quotes a 1990 essay by Antonio D'Alfonso regarding a "third phase [that] will perhaps bring us back to the personal and political realm." By recognizing that a third stage was in fact now active, Clements provides a critical stance that far exceeds what most Italian Canadian critics themselves have been willing to propose.

The major obstacle to a full appreciation of Italian North American writing, both internal and external to the larger communities it encompasses, is the lack of historicization. While some critics suggest that it is a matter of functioning in an environment that offers no tradition, it is important to stress that no hyphenated writer emerges *tabula rasa* from the oyster shell of expatriation. Even if not rooted in North American soil, writers are inscribed by history and carry a catalogue of experience.

Rather than expect to find a ready-made tradition in which to fit, immigrant writers and cultural workers might themselves provide the material construction/collation of a cultural past. The cultures of expatriates may often have been deemed secondary to the official culture of their land of origin, and may have indeed remained unexpressed due to the oppressive nature of national compromise. As such, immigrants, upon arrival in their new home, were/are forced to make a choice which, more often than not, dictates that they must once again suppress their own culture in order to embrace the culture of their host country.

The supposed resolution of the crisis of displacement, as has been suggested by more than one critic, would be through finding, as ambiguous as it may be, a Canadian or American identity. In the Canadian sphere, while official multiculturalism does make overtures to heterogeneity, the general cultural climate blatantly valorizes certain expressions over others. This repeats the activity of the forces of cultural determinism that are at work within the phenomenon of e/im-migration. Multiculturalism tends to facilitate and propagate images of ethnic and minority literatures as nothing more than nostalgic portrayals of the possibility or impossibility of a return to an illusionary rootedness.

Alternative reactions to displacement beyond nostalgia exist within each hyphenated group's expressive spectrum, but these are not what interest the multiculturalist's agenda. The most interesting expression of hyphenated identity comes from the instigation of cultural dialogue, and from the antagonism that it represents for the official culture. Writers such as Antonio D'Alfonso and Caterina Edwards in Canada, and Carole Maso, Vincent Ferrini, and Gilbert Sorrentino in the U.S.A., seek to extend the possibility of dialogue/knowledge to those who undertake the challenge of making a language new to suit their expression.

The work of Italian North American writers often carries within it allusions to cultural products that deflect attention from the works themselves. These "artifacts" are indicative of the necessarily constructive tendency that this sort of writing undertakes. In order to access the threads of these constructions I will begin with Antonio D'Alfonso's novel *Avril ou l'anti-passion* (1990, English trans. *Fabrizio's Passion* 1995).

As D'Alfonso has done previously in *The Other Shore* (1987), in *Fabrizio's Passion* he stresses the denial of English as "a medium of expression." (175) In the original version of the novel this was done in French. In its English translation, the proposed silencing is continually deferred. And, while English as a mode of expression is indeed not abandoned, its power is diminished by hybridizing it with other languages (Italian, French, Guglionese, film, body-language). It is in the very subject matter of the novel, the conceptualization of a film on family history, identity and displacement, that D'Alfonso successfully transcribes English into a representation of the foreign body. History is inscribed in the protagonist and is represented in silence. The text becomes a product of the writer as a regurgitation of the digested and altered inscription.

What is fascinating is that D'Alfonso chooses to represent that inscription in a language distant from the working languages of his critique. "Tienes una cara de campesino"

(176) offers a series of insights into the impossibility of erasing history through language. The layering and hybridization of language as it is spoken through a body not born within it, finally develops into the expressive escape in which language is denied by language.

In her novella *A Whiter Shade of Pale* (1992), Caterina Edwards deals with the nature of self-discovery and historicization through the persona of an archeologist. The work is built around fragments of information and leaves much to the interpretation of these findings. Nothing is complete and resolved. The reader is left to unveil layers of (someone else's) history: a child's sarcophagus (truncated history), an unmatched pair of earrings (discontinuous history). The juxtaposition of one's own unconscious graphia/writing, as represented by the patterns of the archeologist's recurring nosebleeds, to the body of graphic expression of the vanished Etruscans whose remains are being excavated, provides a way of comparing and constructing history.

George's frequent nosebleeds are described as "a random scattering of red dots on a white page" (8). The silent expression of the body that this image engenders threads a series of images and formal elements that go from the novella's title to the various literary quotes placed within the author's writing itself. The red dots appear as a scattering only because, as with Etruscan language, it is not "that their language is indecipherable . . . It is understanding [it] that presents problems, since it is of unknown origin and cannot with certainty be related to any group of known languages" (Edwards 1992, 1). The literary production of Italian Canadian writers is squarely positioned in an uncertain relationship to both English and Italian traditions. For many, both are learned languages of foreign cultures. As such, the writing of Italian Canadians cannot "with certainty be related to any group of known languages." By establishing this type of questioning of languages, Italian Canadian writers cannot but come to the realization that, as the quote from Greek George Seferis' suggests, " . . . those statues are not the fragments. You yourself are the relic" (7).

In the case of Caterina Edwards, her association with the Italian Canadian writing group is particular, since her first identity signifier, her name, does not immediately suggest such an association. Her novella is particularly interesting because of the way in which Edwards continues her experiments with contextualization found in another one of her books, *The Lion's Mouth* (1982). In *A Whiter* the sense of search and construction of context is more explicit. George is attracted to Etruscans precisely because he is unable to contextualize them. He himself seeks a decontextualized existence, a relationship to the world that offers continuously shifting terms of reference and interpretation (40-41). What is left behind or left over from the interpretative work in this novella, are the protuberances of our life and work that have broken off like the noses of the statues from the digs. These are the artifacts that provide a context for those who read our passage. Finally, as with the Etruscan writing that is "read but not understood" (43), one must ask one's self if this is the ethnic experience. Aging and memory (and not the artifacts of George's relationships) are the elements of hidden contextualization that we must decipher. A less explicit and obtrusive writing, whose signs of ethnicity are no less present, would enable us to outline some potential evolutionary trends Italian Canadian writing. In fact, Lesley Clement's terms of reference for her discussion of the "third stage" in Italian Canadian letters are Caterina Edwards and myself.

While I provisionally accept Clements reading of D'Alfonso's "third stage" designation, we should beware of the fact that it is not simply a stage in a progression. This "stage" which may be designated by style and linguistic experimentation exists concurrently with other "stages." What third stage writers illustrate is that no group is reduceable to any particular set of themes and modalities. The appearance of progress, evolution, and definition of stages may be a matter of genera-

tional distinctions or cultural distance from one's place of origins, language of choice, or other such variants, even if these
are but a few of the determinants that influence a body of
work.

For instance, the silence regarding my writing on the part
of the Italian Canadian writing/critical community is directly
related to institutionalized "multiculturalism" and its influence on the prescription of ethnic identity. It designates value according to predefined themes. To act upon language in such a
manner, while not denying the historical basis of English or
Italian, alters these languages so as to emphasize the presence
of an external or dissonant subject. The alteration of English
syntactical sequences, the insertion of Latinate terms, verses or
words in Italian, Neapolitan, Latin, are all meant to instigate a
cultural temblor. No language is privileged, and though English is overwhelmingly more present it is contaminated by the
other languages. This creates a linguistic environment that allows the subject to roam somewhat undetected. And because
the backgrounds of the authors are very different, we cannot
be representative of the same stage in Italian Canadian writing. We are a stageless formation of dissimilar poetics offering
a multipolar critique of our Canadian and Italian realities.

My American Cousin

In his introduction to *Know Fish* (1979) Vincent Ferrini writes
that "the thrust of the whole work is in the title, knowing
fishes, in men, women and the sea" (xix). The allusion is to the
fishing folk and environment of Gloucester. As such, fish are
the optimal element for imaging silent lip movement. Ferrini's
writing is reminiscent of the silence of the men and women
who have no time for poetry, who are involved in the business
of survival. Ferrini does not intend to let these lives pass unnoticed.

"Dis town is our poem n I'ma eets eye," he writes. His
choice of language indicates that he is deeply involved in its

cultural life. He sees "our immigrant past in the livid language of the spoken silences of the fishfolk" (xix). The second and largest section of *Know Fish*, entitled "Da soups," is written in an odd Anglo-Italian (xv), a language that is neither English nor Italian but a hybrid which results from not belonging to either language or culture. These sounds are an attempt at communicating the elements of a culture of migration and work. Ferrini's work stands in testimony to the inventiveness which marginal and minority cultures engage as a mode of survival.

Subaltern groups, displaced as they are within an official or dominant culture, must negotiate a communicative middleground within that relationship. As a cultural interstice this represents the ground for hybridization and hegemonic commerce.

Dream Rida: Henry Ferrini

A hunk ov sod all seed
has tansy fa germaine
da 4 elements have a fifth-
hees house is Indian grain

here's t da wacky pollen
fuckoff stalin

a heraclitus hankerin fa ackshun
selectin ingredients frum da garbage
ah copt out copin with zigzaggin parts
an Eco music on a star bridge

here's t da orphic
all free euphoric! (166)

Another writer whose work calls for further attention from Italian North American critics is Gilbert Sorrentino. It is quite apparent that difficulties plague certain critics when they approach works that offer no easily attainable signs of ethnicity.

Too many still depend on explicit social realistic representations as markers of difference and refute all else out-of-hand. They do more harm than good to the very field they supposedly want to enhance. In fact, these critics feed stereotypical typologies with their emphasis on clearly definable types and customs.

Many of Sorrentino's works contain Italian characters that are somewhat at odds with the "American" linguistic environment in which they are set. Aside from the fact of their names and sometimes accented expression, Sorrentino's Italians do not impose their ethnicity. In one of his own essays dedicated to discussing his background and how it influences his work, Gilbert Sorrentino makes a case for an invisible code that threads through his writing. "I am, most hopelessly, an American writer, but my formal concerns are rooted in my hereditary makeup, so that my Americanism is one of the material to hand" (Sorrentino 1984, 265).

The Italian characters that populate Sorrentino's works are not inactive or merely present. While some apparently represent "the formal concerns [that] are rooted in [their] hereditary makeup," like the Reccos in *Aberration of Starlight* (1980), others offer more consciously critical ethnic presences. The most intriguing of these is Dr. Ciccarelli in *Blue Pastoral* (1983), whose accented language alerts other to his identity. Perceived through his accent, Ciccarelli ingeniously uses it, among other things, as a tool to manipulate others who take such traits as indicative of cultural inferiority or intellectual inefficacy. At one point in the novel, Ciccarelli drops his accented speech and begins an explication of its function:

> Wait! We are in a slight dilemma, good Doc. Somehow, that, uh, how shall we say, stage "greaseball" accent, direct from the beloved Hollywood "films" of the 30s and 40s, has disappeared from your speech. It makes one . . . Think . . . Ha ha! How delightful that you've noticed. That is my — I like to call it my —

"golden-earring-and-drooping mustachio" accent. It works wonders with idiot WASPs from the clamorous plains and environs, especially when employed at sidewalk feasts like those of St. Anthony, San Gennaro, and Santa Rosalia, by Italo-Americans, all of whom are Ph.D.s. With the accent, a few shrugs and hand-talk, and that white smile preceding the well-known and beloved infectious laugh, my countrymen get rid of mountains of eighth-rate "food" that would ordinarily be used to bait rat traps. Also useful in shilling "games" of — ho ho — "chance." It is my warm accent, my winnig accent, my I-am-so- grateful accent, my great-big-family accent. It is the accent used when some poor contadino is queried by the police as to the source of a few hundred grand in cash found in an old AWOL bag. You get the idea, right? Works something like that other famous speech tic, the brogue. But enough ethnicity! (7)

Sorrentino seems to suggest that ethnicity, and its affiliated stereotypical assignations, can be turned on and off without risking one's identity in the game. For ethnicity, as Dr. Ciccarelli explicates, is literally a put-on, something that is "put on" others by those who designate ethnicity, or may be "put on" by individuals much in the manner that Ciccarelli does. Ethnicity becomes here an element that can be defined in fairly straightforward terms, and that, in fact, has nothing to do with one's identity or culture. In this case, Sorrentino's sense of ethnicity finds affinity with Ferrini's vision of it as inventive, practical and somewhat deceptive. Ethnicity is presented as a tool that is used to put outsiders off their track. This layering of realities, that Sorrentino defines in the above quoted essay as the general signifying marker of Italian art, is also the term by which it enables "ethnics" to shield their lives from the scrutiny of outsiders.

Carol Maso's novels expand linguistic and compositional innovation beyond the merely illustrative and narrative. Her language is in an apparent state of constant undoing. It is, in fact, the expansion of a narrative voice into polyphony. A sample of this is to be found in the first few pages of the novel *Ava*. There Maso unveils what takes place in the use of spare language:

> Just once I'd like to save Virginia Woolf from drowning. Hart Crane. Primo Levi from falling. Paul Celan, Bruno Schultz, Robert Desnos, and for my parents: Grandma and Grandpa, Uncle Isaac, Uncle Solly, Aunt Sophie, just once . . . In the city of New York. Where I taught school, sang songs, watched my friends come and go. Climbed the pointy buildings. Marveled at all the light . . . Aldo, building cathedrals with his voice . . . A man in a bowler hat disappears into thin air. Grandfather . . . She was dressed in a gown of gold satin. Suppose it had been me? . . . She shudders at the sight of a garter belt as if it were a contraption of supreme torture . . . I think of him often: Samuel Beckett learning to fly . . . Look for this in my shoe . . . He waits for disguised contacts who sometimes never come . . . A a. B b . . . All the bodies piling up on stage . . . C . . . Like your father you grew old roses . . . Snow falls like music in the late autumn . . . Home, before it was divided. (20-21)

Maso intertwines memories with the present, with dreams and activity, with everyday events and natural phenomena. These are, afterall, the things that touch our lives and form the narratives of identity.

The undeniable resistance to Zanzotto and Villa's work in the anglophone world, detectable in the dearth of available translations, is indicative of the threat that unassimilable difference represents in the literary realm. This, coupled with the trajectory of their poetic experimentation, provides a viable and valuable example for Italians writing within the context of other cultures.

Italian North American writers are to some extent tied to traditions of both the host culture and the ones they left behind. Poetics that undo the romantic notion of a standardized Italian language and culture as being the predominant model to which some Italian North American writers aspire are essential for the liberation of Italians abroad from the cultural imposition of a national ideology that created their condition. A frontal approach must be taken in relation to the fictions that propagate the illusion of an essential Italian character. Italianità is a cultural remnant that must be given its proper context as an inhibitor of the diversity that Italian immigrants throughout the world represent. The poetics illustrated herein are but a few of the valuable emerging methodologies that go toward the acquisition of agency for the post-emigrant subject. These authors and their works create a space where silence can be heard as a function of speech and a condition that is beginning to break:

> when the structure breaks
> the rescue
> motion into coherence.

Tracing the Ground of Identity

Ethnicity and Race in Women's Narratives

> How easy it is to lose sight of what is historically invisible — as if people lived only history and nothing else . . . To the underprivileged, home is represented, not by a house, but by a practice or set of practices. Everyone has his own. These practices, chosen and not imposed, offer in their repetition, transient as they may be in themselves, more permanence, more shelter than any lodging. Home is no longer a dwelling but the untold story of a life being lived. At its most brutal, home is no more than one's name — whilst to most people one is nameless.
>
> John Berger
> *And Our Faces, My Heart, Brief as Photos*

The facile categorization of people and practices that plagues our everyday reflects the inattention afforded the truly pluricultural makeup of our society. The conventional "application form," with its definitions of ethnicity, among which is the category of "other," can only represent a momentary illusion of proper and proportional representation. While "white" cannot in any way be regarded an ethnicity, it has nevertheless become the fulcrum upon which issues of race and ethnicity are articulated in day-to-day affairs and in scholarly discourse. As constructs that vary in space and time, race and ethnicity are anything but secure categories. Nevertheless, their function is exactly one of security, where differentiation seems to provide the minimum amount of comfort for those who strictly deem themselves unlike others.

In the context of emigration, acculturation, assimilation and nation, ethnicity and race are plastic elements that are not conceptually linked to descendency, pigmentation, and other similarly favored somatic markers. Most importantly, these are all distinct expressions of cultural and ideological construction. As such, it follows that those who have fallen between the cracks of a multicultural debate predicated by issues of race and color have skillfully been manipulated to serve as examples of assimilation and success in "American" society. Unless we want to equate assimilation with an absence of history, and therefore give-up the possibility of finding ways in which to understand the process of cultural erasure, I believe that the place of historical ethnicity in the narratives of Italian North American women writers might be one among many useful points of reference.

These writings represent an effort to offer an alternative reading of a condition that has either been forgotten, because deemed assimilated into "whiteness," or one that is regarded merely as subsisting in still stereotyped representations along the treacherous road of identity. Though not a lot has been said or written on the issue of race and ethnicity in relation to Italian North Americans, it is imperative that this issue, one that is intimately tied to the history of Italian emigration, be raised again and again.[1] Be it the product of first, second, or successive generations, much of Italian North American writing can be better understood by positioning it within the history of the formation of the Italian nation and the history of immigration in countries such as Canada and Germany. The recuperation of the conditioning rhetoric of specific historical periods can provide useful critical tools and help to improve the current dynamics that dictate ethnic and race relations not only in the U.S.A. and Canada, but throughout the world.

Racial, ethnic, and cultural distinctions emphasized within Italian Risorgimento and post-Unification literature served to establish a "natural" hierarchy by which a large portion of the peninsular population, namely that of the South and the Islands, came to be regarded as non-Italian, foreign and racially inferior.[2] These negative appellations of ethnic and racial difference followed emigrants to North America. While somewhat dissipated and negated by Italians themselves in order to avoid association with more socially disadvantaged sectors of the population these definitions still function in the popular mind to maintain less than favorable perceptions of Italians. F. James Davis, in *Who is Black?: One Nation's Definition* (1991) notes that

> in *The Passing of the Great Race* (1916), Madison Grant maintained that the one-drop rule should be applied not only to blacks but also to all other ethnic groups he considered biologically inferior "races," such as Hindus, Asians in general, Jews, Italians, and other Southern and Eastern European peoples. Grant . . . and others succeeded in getting Congress to pass the national origins quota laws of the early 1920s. This racist quota legislation sharply curtailed immigration from everywhere in the world except Northern and Western Europe and the Western Hemisphere, until it was repealed in 1965.(13)
>
> . . . He warned against the alleged unscrupulousness of the Polish Jew, the inferiority of Italians and immigrants from other nations of Southern and Eastern Europe, and the horrors of an ethnic melting pot. (27)

In recent years the efficacy and historical accuracy of the accepted "whiteness" of Italians has been questioned by Italian North American women artists and writers. Two of the most visible and controversial individuals to address and problematize this question have been Madonna and Camille Paglia. Aside from the merits or inadequacies of Madonna and Paglia's explorations of the conventions of whiteness and their detractors' reactions, it is mostly the ambivalence that their body of work emphasizes in the realm of ethnicity and race that has generated such strong responses. Neither mamma Ciccone nor Ms. Paglia engage either black or white identity politics, and on top of that they sell anti-feminist feminism. One is a performer who doubles as cultural commentator, and the other is an academic whose lectures fall into the realm of performance art.

No matter how we might feel about their social commentary, these two Italian American women cannot be ignored. Camille Paglia exalts what she refers to as "Italian pagan Catholicism," which allows her the option of being either adhering or irreverent toward culture and society. But this is only the tip of the iceberg. Paglia celebrates a particular kind of "sophisticated European sexuality of a kind we have not seen since the great foreign films of the 1950s and 1960s" (calling to mind such actresses such as Anna Magnani and Sofia Loren). She praises Elizabeth Taylor who "in 1958, [as] a raven-haired vixen and temptress took Eddie Fisher away from Debbie Reynolds and became a pariah of the American press . . . As an Italian, I saw that a battle of cultures was under way: antiseptic American blondeness was being swamped by a rising tide of sensuality, a new force that would sweep my Sixties generation into open rebellion" (Paglia 1992, 15).

Paglia's identification with a darker presence in society and on screen leads her to consider the work of Madonna. Paglia identifies the sources of Madonna's performance styles as what the singer/dancer "ha[s] taken from urban blacks, Hispanics, and her own middle-class but turbulent and charismatic Italian-American family" (6). The last element of this quote is irritating by its italicizing act, one that emphasizes and makes Italians a middle-ground element in the discourse on race. To present Italians as potentially a profoundly important presence in the psyche and imaginary of part of the greater population, offends both poles of the Black and White race equation.

Furthermore, this ambivalence offers little assurance of steady alliances to either side. Italians have on the whole been guilty of exploiting this situation in order to assimilate. Yet their attempt at integration and assimilation has been frustrated by the fact that America's "white" social hierarchy is a limited enrollment club, certainly with regard to Italians who maintain a strong attachment to their cultural peculiarities generation after generation.

The odd position held by Italians in North American societies is illustrated by the fact that while they recognize their only partial acceptance into American society, they nevertheless, as Spike Lee's films *Jungle Fever* and *Do the Right Thing* dramatize, often form the front-line resistance to the expansion of African Americans into white society.[3] Italians seem to have accepted this position and have let themselves fall into a powerless state that separates them from both sides of the colour spectrum.

As a result, Madonna's African American influenced work is deemed as exploitative appropriation, and her "blond ambition" phase as a manifestation of wanna-be-whiteism, rather than a critique and manipulation of "blonde ambition." Paglia suggests that "Madonna's most enduring cultural contribution may be that she has introduced ravishing visual beauty and a lush Mediterranean sensuality into parched, pinched, word-drunk Anglo-Saxon feminism" (13). It is somewhat unfortunate that while Madonna offends puritanical WASPS she also troubles some African Americans by appearing to usurp Black sensuality. Another question however must be brought up regarding this split identity: aside from the appropriation of black elements as points of recognition for some Italian Americans, what are some of the elements internal to our community and history that require further exploration of issues associated with race? Some of the answers to this question are provided by the writings of number of Italian North American women.

The works that follow, while related to Madonna and Paglia's aim to problematize "whiteness," complicate their critique by addressing other pertinent issues: sexuality, race relations, the creation of alliances, and reproduction rights.[4] Rose Romano, Dodici Azpadu, Mary (Bucci) Bush and Mary Melfi, all of whom have articulated questions of race and ethnicity in their work, deserve more critical attention, if we are not to lose sight of what is historically invisible.[5]

Invisibility is a central theme in the writings of Rose Romano. In her essay "Coming Out Olive in the Lesbian Community: Big Sister is Watching You," Romano's critique is aimed at the Lesbian community:

> I have been censored in the lesbian press and ostracized in the lesbian community because I call myself Olive. Politically correct lesbians have agreed with the division of people into two categories: white and "of color." I look white; therefore I am white. There is no distinction made between different groups within the white community — if I am white, I am assigned wasp history and culture . . . I have been told that by calling myself Olive I am evading my "responsibility of guilt" (Loriggio 1996, 161-162).

However, as the following section from the poem "Dago Street" demonstrates (Romano 1994), Romano undermines external attempts at constructing her experience as conforming to a ready-made identity. The poem points to contradictions inherent in most "discussions of racism" to the silent spaces left without expression:

> After a discrete look around
> at another discussion of racism
> in the lesbian community

I chose her
and settled down to wait.
There was the Mexican woman
who was enraged to be asked
whether it was safe to travel to Mexico.
I know that pain.
They tell me it's not worth
the risk of going to Sicily
to look for my family.
There was the Jewish woman
who was horrified to be told
to forget the Holocaust.
I know that pain.
They tell me it's pointless and
morbid to think about the lynchings.
There was the Black woman
who was shocked to be advised to
pass, to ensure her own survival
through cultural suicide.
I know that pain.
They tell me I have white skin privilege. (22)

Dodici Azpadu's first novel, *Saturday Night in the Prime of Life* (1986) is a subtle illustration of the silencing of Southern Italian history. The author's jacket note states that she seeks "to nourish appreciation for the neglected and ignored non-white qualities of Sicilian character." In opposition to Azpadu's statement, further participating in the silencing of the voice Azpadu seeks to make heard, is the publisher's note, which paradoxically observes that "though primarily Neddie and Lindy's story, the context of the novel — the trap — is the male dominated Sicilian culture that affects the women who exist inside and outside of it." The novel tells the story of Sicilian American Neddie and her WASP lover Lindy, and of their attempt to maintain a relationship despite familial opposition. Neddie is attached to her Sicilian culture, which she considers to be a signifier of racial otherness. "The trap" that Azpadu reveals is the status of Sicilians in the eyes of non-Sicilians. The negative effects of Sicilian culture and identity are nothing more than the prejudices and misconceptions that Lindy and her parents harbor.

When planning a meeting with her parents, Lindy asks herself if "she [had] even mentioned to them that Neddie was Sicilian" (23). While Neddie's family is hopelessly bigoted with regards to Neddie's sexuality, Lindy's family is more preoccupied with Neddie's ethnic identity. Lindy knew

> her parents suspected that this person called Neddie was actually a man . . . If they never met again, she thought, her parents might prefer not to see the obvious in Neddie . . . But even if they could ignore that, could they also ignore what was obvious in her deeply olive complexion, her wiry hair, her face and hand language? (23)

Lindy, too, shares somewhat in her parents' dislike for Sicilians:

> [Lindy] knew the Zingaros only from snapshots and stories, and from their effect on Neddie's life and on her own life . . . [Neddie's mother's] nose, eyes and mouth epitomized an unpleasant racial mixing which only in Neddie did Lindy find attractive . . . How could she love Sicilian ways in Neddie, yet dislike them in Neddie's family? (29-30)

Further, it is the uncertainty of her own ability to set aside her prejudiced view of Sicilians that also precipitates much of the imbalance within Lindy's relationship with Neddie.

> Aren't there ways to help her keep that blood circulating without relying on family ties; Lindy felt the

inadequacy that always discouraged her. Racial comfort was what Concetta could give that she could not.
Neddie will consider leaving me (62).

Neddie's struggle with her family is the mirror image of her relationship with Lindy; it is not about breaking from Sicilian
culture, but it is a struggle with her family to achieve acceptance for her sexuality. Lindy, on the other hand, while aware
of the power of Neddie's Sicilian identity, is blind to her own
inability to accept Neddie as such.

Azpadu's short story "Desert Ruins," included in the anthology *The Voices We Carry* (Bona, 1994) is another explicit
expression of the need to state identity for one's self, often
against extreme external opposition. One of the protagonists,
Marco, encapsulates Sicilian history by the statement that "if
the genocide of a people is more or less accomplished . . . as is
the case of indigenous Sicilians, neither the fact of genocide
nor the remaining people themselves has any standing" (194).
The most important aspect of this statement and Marco's per-
sistence is that it extends recognition to others. The self-
awareness Marco displays functions as a way to construct alliances with other similarly affected groups. His statement of
identity is also one of solidarity and admiration for John Be-
gay, a Native American activist. And, if identity politics is to be
of any value, it must be in the establishment of a politics of mu-
tual recognition and in the building of alliances and coalitions.[6]

Mary Bush's coalition-building is achieved in matters of
race and ethnicity by placing Italian immigrants and Blacks
side by side: they work the same land, and struggle under the
same economic hardships. While we cannot expect to find the
experience of both groups equal (the history of slavery continues to condition the existence of African Americans), we cannot overlook the historiographical record of Italian immigrants
to North America.

In the story "Drowning," two young girls, Isola and Dotsey, one Italian the other Black, are daughters of plantation workers in the American South. They spend their days together. Their shared experiences are tempered by an uncertain alliance. After one of the Italian workers finds himself in trouble, and is hunted down by the plantation owner's men, Isola is told by her parents to stay away from the man's daughter. The following conversation takes place between Isola and Dotsey:

> If we play with Nina the Americans will shoot us. Or maybe burn down our "house." . . . Dotsey put her hands on her hips. "You dumb or something? White folks don't shoot white folks." . . . "But we're not white," Isola told her. "We're Italian." (Bucci Bush 1995, 11)

Isola's statement of solidarity, whether conscious or naive, is nevertheless a telling reflection of her family's and other Italians' view of themselves. Of course, such alliances are always put to the test. After witnessing the rape of Dotsey's cousin, Lecie, by Mr. Horton, a white Company man, Dotsey's reaction, though predictable, is surprising. She must side with her cousin against oppression and abuse. After Lecie's rape Dotsey apparently cannot bring herself to fully trust Isola. Therefore, at the story's end, when Isola tries to follow Dotsey home, the problem of the complexity of race relations fully unfolds:

> Dotsey turned around and looked back at Isola. "Stupid," she called over her shoulder. "Stupid Dago." Then she ran home. (22)

This is an extremely revealing circumstance. The status and position of Italian North Americans, and the depth and problematics of integration and assimilation, are illustrated by this incident. Having been shunned by Dotsey, Isola feels the pull of assimilation. She wants to let go of a piece of herself that apparently no longer has a place in the social equation. As such, a question has emerged as a central issue in the writing of many Italians abroad that in its denial has also had deep and lasting effects on the psyche of many immigrants.

Mary Melfi, whose novel *Infertility Rites* (1991) highlights circumstances tied to a more traditional environment involving issues of motherhood and reproduction, also proposes an investigation into the conflicted realm of assimilation and identity. Fertility, once a positive trait within traditional societies, has in contemporary terms come to be regarded as a curse and used against women as a means of control and exclusion within the family, in work, and in education. Melfi's formula goes beyond the politics of reproduction and includes issues of ethnic and minority identity, as well as cultural critique, and self-reflective passage. Throughout the novel, she equates blackness with fertility and the assimilated (or non-black) with infertility. Whiteness and infertility correspond to success. Struggle is defined as a strategy by which blackness and fertility are both valorized.

Feelings of ethnic inadequacy and attempts at integration clash. While the protagonist Nina reflects that her "failure to get pregnant fills [her] whole life with failure," fertility, or being successful in getting pregnant, is considered as giving-in to "mestissage," diluting ethnicity. Not that Nina feels a strong tie to any country or population ("Fighting for my only country, my body" 86), she is nevertheless strongly conditioned by her background and by the prescribed identity as an ethnic in the Canadian mosaic. Nina nicely reads this Mosaic and her place within it: "that is why I am always out of place in the Canadian mosaic: I have a chip on my shoulder . . . " (56), by which she also displaces her position as a chip in the mosaic to a source of conflict.

Dysfunctional and a divided person in the novel, Nina is surrounded by friends, Mary, Diana, and her own mother, who are nothing more than dimensions of her other selves. The miscarriages and infertility that Nina suffers are at odds with her needs to "create a new country out of an old one"

(13). She finds a way to define identity without giving in to prescribed notions of what she is: the artist and traveler, the daughter, wife and (failed) mother, the "black" immigrant and the assimilated middle-class "white" woman. Above all, Nina is in search of the right to be herself in her various manifestations. At this point the double meaning of the title comes strongly into play. *Infertility Rites* also reads as infertility rights. The condition of fertility appears to be one dictated by choice, a choice of the body that must resolve its uncertain alliances. Infertility becomes a way to protest and question one's background and the move toward assimilation, both of which are directly related to questions of nationalism and identity:

> "Didn't you feel at home in Italy? You're bilingual," I add, knowing how involved she was in the Italian community — president of her hometown's association (the youngest ever elected).
> "I did, but when I was asked What nationality are you? I never hesitated to answer Canadian. Italo-Canadian — nah? Just plain and simple: Canadian."
> "Well, it goes to show you that even this country, famous for its dullness, can brainwash its children. It did the job on us." Sarcastic, equating nationalism with childhood conditioning. (75)

Melfi's strategy is to turn the acceptance of infertility into an option that leads back to fertility. That is a strategy that includes the trajectories proposed by the other writers mentioned. When not an imposed condition, fertility becomes an important trope by which to emphasize ethnicity or "blackness." Culture as fertility, when rescued from disappearance, becomes acceptable as a way to re-establish the worth of non-assimilated traditions and cultures. Fertility and culture, almost synonymous terms in which the writers herein participate in illustrating through their mutually applicable adaptability and resilience.

Fante's Inferno

Ask the Dust
and the Sins of Representation

I come to John Fante not as an Americanist but as an Italianist, a reader conditioned by his readings in Italian literature. The background to this paper is further provided by my work in the history, sociology, and culture of Italian e/im-migration. And, as an Italian immigrant myself, I must read texts such as John Fante's through that very specific personal filter that is hard to deny. These brief initial comments come uncomfortably close to the sensitive borders of "identity politics." In answer to any preoccupations regarding the ambivalent relationship that many have to these words in quotation marks I will only ask: What else but through identity do we, any one of us, read, write or live? Excluding or ignoring the fact of John Fante's Italian American identity with experiences that were a direct result of that identity, and that his characters (not always, but more often than not) are representative of those experiences, personal or observed, is indeed a serious omission.

The preceding remarks find especially favorable ground if we consider the social position of Italian immigrants to North America in the early days of influx and the relationships of those immigrants and their successive generations to "American" society. Especially when we concern ourselves with immigrants from the Southern regions of Italy, which made up three-quarters of all immigrants from Italy, one important aspect conditioning of their social position, aside from the obvious class differences with those not regarded as e/im-migrants, is the construction of those populations as racially different from the Italian population. The legacy of the works of Cesare Lombroso, Alfredo Niceforo, Giuseppe Sergi, and other positivist scientists of the turn of the century, who defined Southern Italians as inferior beings along with Jews and Africans, has had a long lasting effect on views of Southerners in Italy itself. However, these views were easily exported and apparently indiscriminately applied to Italian immigrants abroad, working to make of them less than desirable citizens in places like the U.S.A. and Canada. In the former, the immigration exclusion laws of the 1920s, that were brought into play as a result of Madison Grant's exhortations and warnings regarding the threat to American "purity" that the influx of inferior races presented, included Italians as well as Asian and Eastern European populations. Fante demonstrates in his work, and especially in *Ask the Dust,* that he is painfully aware of the problems that Italians faced in the U.S.A. during his time.

Since this is not the forum to develop the aspects of race construction regarding Southern Italians and Italian immigrants to the U.S.A., I offer it here as a point of departure. Fante must be read as someone most likely painfully aware of ethnic and racial injustice in the U.S.A. His approach at condemning it is indirect and runs the risk of being regarded as racist itself. Rather, I would term it honest, direct, and disturbing. Injustice and racism are disturbing. A straight-out and conventional condemnation of them would be too simple and relieve the reader of the disturbance that racism may cause. But that's not Fante's way. He wants his writing to upset and disturb, he seeks to shake readers out of any comfortable and illusory distance we might assume. For this reason, I believe that his unfinished controversial work *Little Brown Brothers,* that few have seen but of which we hold a published sample in "Helen, Thy Beauty Is to Me" (*The Wine of Youth,* 1989), would make an important contribution to the understanding of Fante's relationship to race relations, ethnicity, and the way in which "appropriation of voice" may be regarded as an aid for the communication of an unspoken and possibly repressed history, rather than a mere erasure of the appropriated voice. *Ask the Dust* is a step, a very important step, in that direction.

Finally, I would like to conclude this introduction by engaging Fante in the cultural continuum that I believe is formed by the extension of Italian culture to include its expatriate components. Fante is undoubtedly an American writer, because the American experience is so much about displacement and alienation, and he is most definitely an Angeleno by condition. Yet he is no less Italian because of these other identities. In fact, he may be even more Italian as a result of them. In any case, we would have no trouble finding parallels or a context for John Fante within Italian literature. The names that come to mind immediately are Cesare Pavese and Elio Vittorini, and Pier Paolo Pasolini is not so distant a soul-mate. By the same token, and to bring it full circle to other writers working within the Italian North American experience, Fante finds extension and even fulfillment in writers such as Gay Talese in *Unto the Sons* (Knopf, 1992), Antonio D'Alfonso in *Fabrizio's Passion* (Guernica, 1995), and Mary Bucci Bush in *Drowning* (Parentheses, 1995); or even in the films and writings of Abel Ferrara and Quentin Tarantino.

Whatever the case may be, John Fante is expressive of what I would like to call *the preclusion of representation.* Taken beyond the possibility of speaking for those that did not speak for themselves, Fante speaks to his characters' acquaintances in the voices that perforated the souls of those he loved. The invectives thrown out by characters like Bandini are those that have been flung at him, which he has gathered in an attempt to cast them far from himself.

Charles Bukowski's introduction to the 1980 edition of *Ask the Dust* quotes it as being representative of John Fante's "magic" (6), and characterizes Fante and the "way of his words and the way of his way [as being] the same: strong and good and warm" (7). But, as contemporary readers inflected by the demands of particular problems of representation as issued from both conservative and progressive camps, we must ask more, and in different ways, of texts such as *Ask the Dust*. I am referring in particular to the relationship established within the pages of that novel between the fledgling writer Arturo Bandini and the apparent object of his desires, the waitress at the Columbia Buffet, Camilla Lopez. Here, on the surface of it at least, in the relationship of this writer and the Mexican waitress, there is nothing "strong and good and warm" but only weakness, pettiness and the coldness of hypocrisy and ignorance, unless we let the surface lead us to the depths. That we in fact must require more of texts such as *Ask the Dust* is not to say that they cannot provide answers to the new questions posed. It is too easy to dismiss *Ask the Dust* as racist, sexist, or otherwise tag it as superfluous. The fact is that such texts invite a questioning and re-examination of themselves through evolving paradigms that marks them as infinitely relevant.

John Fante's greatest technique and signifier, and most likely the device that aids those who seek to easily categorize his work, is indirection (or misdirection). In many ways *Ask the Dust* falls into that tradition of love poetry that seeks to gaze upon its object of desire by averting its glance in fear of disrupting the integrity and intensity of the felt desire. This aversion (in all senses of the word) threatens the identity of the desired one, even to the detriment of any immediate relationship that might arise. Dante and Beatrice, Petrarca and Laura: the poets' attention to disguise their gaze, the tradition that valorizes the function of a screen through which to re-direct desire toward the appropriate yet restricted body, also touches Fante's work, though to different ends. Our problems as contemporary readers begin with relationships of desire which, as defined by a great deal of literature, are most often ones of subjection, appropriation, and dismissal of the appropriate values inherent in the subject upon which the desiring gaze is cast.

While here I do not intend to contextualize Fante in terms of any literary tradition, I find that the proposition of these similarities allows renewed opportunity to read Fante's works. Fante requires inclusion within a discourse of multiculturalism that tests assumed notions of what comports that concept and its applications.

Texts such as *Ask the Dust* place John Fante in an odd predicament. Under accusations of racism, and that he demeans the minorities portrayed within his works, Fante should be castigated as the product of a less enlightened era and attitudes, as the representative of a mainstream, white dominated literary establishment that works to the detriment, and the maintainment at a lowly status, of minorities and, as such, be undeserving of our attention. And yet Fante cannot be held in any of these categories if we can give his work a particular attention that looks at the tensions between individuals within the texts as the beginnings, rather than the ends, of our readings.

Fante was far from mainstream, and received less than encouraging support from the literary establishment. Categorizations such as "white" overlook the historical construction of many groups that have been absorbed by that very category. As to his mode of representation of minorities, this is a topic that needs to be addressed more than I will do here, merely in the hope of at least opening a dialogue with those who have tended to dismiss him. In this case, *Ask the Dust* is doubly fruitful for its explicit self-reflectiveness regarding the subject of representation and identity, and illustratively for how the modes involving such processes are rather complex and convoluted.

This wonderfully compact and misleadingly simple text is a narrative dealing with the perceived need to transform one's self into an image that will deny one's historical reality.

As such, it is packed with contradictory and conflictual messages, the end product of which is to short-circuit the very processes it initiates. Bandini wants to be an Italian who is "a credit to the Italian people," like Joe DiMaggio (11), whom he mentions at the open of his novel. Yet, when he begins to define his place, Bandini can only do so through his imagination:

> I saw myself a great author with that natty Italian briar, and a cane, stepping out of a big black car, and she was there too, proud as hell of me, the lady in the silver fox fur . . . A day and another day and the day before, and the library with the big boys in the shelves, old Dreiser, old Mencken, all the boys down there, and I went to see them, Hya Dreiser, Hya Mencken, Hya, hya: there's a place for me too, and it begins with B, in the B shelf, Arturo Bandini, make way for Arturo Bandini, his slot for his book, and I sat at the table and just looked at the place where my book would be . . . (13)

Bandini works hard to deny his background and the fact that he does not fit into the society that he describes. The places Bandini occupies, the run-down cafes and cheap hotels are the places to which Italians of his background are relegated. His denial of this fact must necessarily include the demeaning of anything associated with that world and that might possibly tie him to it, such as Camilla. Is she the culmination of a racist desire for "a Mexican girl?" (15) No doubt Bandini is rather simplistic in the application of his stereotypes, or could it be that it was a true attraction to girls who reminded him of Italian girls, and that the attraction he imagined to the "lady in the silver fox fur" was due to the pressures of assimilation? These are some of the sins Bandini must exculpate. Not to be redeemed by some higher force, but to undo the pattern that his denials cause him to relive repeatedly by his actions and by self-doubt. Castigated in the Dantean *contrappasso,* by which one suffers the punishment represented by the sin, Arturo Bandini trans-

forms his punishment into merely a part of his unshakable being and identity. As he finds, Bandini cannot escape his
identity by denying others. His attempt to do so only brings
the conflict into play even more emphatically. As a result,
Bandini's failure to become "a credit to the Italian people" is a
result of his denial of difference by emphasizing the difference
of others, rather than any particular flaw or inadequacy. His
real sin, one he does not wholly recognize as such, is to erase
the identity of the author of "The Little Dog that Laughed"
and "The Long Lost Hills," short stories he publishes as the
novel evolves. Bandini perceives, in his dream world, these
works as the product of a generic "great author." Camilla, on
the other hand, is a presence that challenges him to gravitate
toward a personalized identity as a writer, one that is in direct
relation with his being Italian (what in effect he wants to be)
and his class.

> Lying in my bed I thought about them, watched the
> blobs of red light from the St. Paul Hotel jump in and
> out of my room, and I was miserable, for tonight I had
> acted like them. Smith and Parker and Jones, I had
> never been one of them. Ah, Camilla! When I was a
> kid back home in Colorado it was Smith and Parker
> and Jones who hurt me with the hideous names, called
> me Wop and Dago and Greaser, and their children
> hurt me, just as I hurt you tonight. They hurt me so
> much I could never become one of them, drove me to
> books, drove me within myself, drove me to run away
> from that Colorado town, and sometimes, Camilla,
> when I see their faces I feel the hurt all over again, the
> old ache there, and sometimes I am glad they are here,
> dying in the sun, uprooted, tricked by their heartless-
> ness, the same faces, the same set, hard mouths, faces
> from my home town, fulfilling the emptiness of their
> lives under a blazing sun.

I see them in the lobbies of hotels, I see them sunning in the parks, and limping out of ugly little churches, their faces bleak from proximity with their strange gods, out of Aimee's Temple, out of the Church of the Great I Am.

I have seen them stagger out of their movie palaces and blink their empty eyes in the face of reality once more, and stagger home, to read the Times, to find out what's going on in the world. I have vomited at their newspapers, read their literature, observed their customs, eaten their food, desired their women, gaped at their art. But I am poor, and my name ends with a soft vowel, and they hate me and my father, and my father's father, and they would have my blood and put me down, but they are old now, dying in the sun and in the hot dust of the road, and I am young and full of hope and love for my country and my times, and when I say Greaser to you it is not my heart that speaks, but the quivering of an old wound, and I am ashamed of the terrible thing I have done. (46-47)

In this confession, Bandini opens up to an absent Camilla and sheds light on the lie he lives as a reaction to the treatment he has suffered. The lies that have been heaped upon him regarding his non-identity as a "real American," he has taken to heart and now repeats against Camilla: "All that paint on your face. You look awful — a cheap imitation of an American. You look frowzy. If I were a Mexican I'd knock your head off. You're a disgrace to your people." (122)

She, however, is not so easily undone:

"Who are you to talk like that?" she said. "I'm just as much an American as you are. Why, you're not an

> American at all. Look at your skin. You're dark like
> Eyetalians. And your eyes, they're black."
> "Brown," I said.
> "They're not either. They're black. Look at your hair.
> Black."
> "Brown," I said. (122)

This passage points to the inability to resolve the shifting paradox of identity in the U.S.A. While diversity is supposedly valued, the demands of assimilation tend toward the very erasure
of diversity. During this exchange Bandini's statement that
Camilla is a "disgrace to [her] people" also provides the ob-
verse of his previous statement about being "a credit to [his]
people." In this instance the matter of identity and relationship to a particular community becomes blurred: Camilla is
American but Mexican, and Bandini is American but Italian.
Of course, the question that is always obtrusively present is: a
credit to which people? Camilla appears to be aware of Bandini's dilemma and his attempts to have it both ways, be an
American who can be a "credit to his people" as an Italian.
This is the impasse of American citizenship. And, drawn as he
is to wanting to assimilate, as he has intimated by his view of
California and the people who populate the Golden State, he
despises the group to which he aspires. He knows he cannot be
one of them, and yet he also denies the traits that Camilla
points out that distinguish him from being what might be
thought of as quintessentially "American," dark eyes and dark
hair.

Bandini's inability to be intimate with Camilla stems
from his direct identification with her. The reasons he is attracted to her are also the reasons he must despise her.

> She opened her arms and all of her seemed to open to
> me, but it only closed me deeper into myself, carrying
> with me the image of her at that time, how lush and
> soft she was.

"Look," I said. "I'm busy. Look." I patted the pile of manuscript beside the typewriter.

"You're afraid, too."

"Of what?"

"Me."

"Pooh."

Silence.

"There's something wrong with you," she said.

"What?"

"You're queer."

I got up and stood over her.

"That's a lie," I said. (123)

This back and forth strongly suggests that the nature of Bandini's attraction to Camille might be self-reflexive. In that case, the "queerness" gives weight for the young man's image of himself in a gendered manner. The apparent rape attempt that follows this exchange hints at the gendered nature of exclusion that Bandini is attempting to overcome or violate. Women are presented throughout Fante's opus as the beings that most affect the young writer, whether it's his mother, or here Camilla, or Vera Rivken. It is women who are for him a mirror of marginality. The men that populate Bandini's world are, at least in his view, weaklings, drunkards, ineffectual, impotent; traits he fears and discovers again and again within himself. In fact, the writer Sammy, who despises Camilla offers another mirror through which Bandini can be self-reflexive. It is through Sammy that Bandini is led to appreciate Camilla's desperation and the elements that he had previously seen as signifiers of failure: "From sand and cactus we Americans had carved an empire. Camilla's people had had their chance. They had failed" (44).

Yet, at the novel's conclusion, Bandini carries his words "a hundred yards into the desolation" (165) among the sand and cactus. Bandini is a changed man no longer struggling to be himself and understands that there is no reason to fear the dust that throughout the novel has had a stifling effect. Now he can ask the dust and not take silence as antagonism. The desert becomes the shelf upon which Bandini sets his story next to Camilla Lopez.

The crisis of identity in Fante's *Ask the Dust* takes place in a split economy of gender and ethnicity. Throughout the pages of the novel there is an undoing of a bitterly reactive subject toward a reconfiguration of a man, an Italian American man, a presence who can finally be "a credit to" Bandini himself.

There Dago!

'Tooning into Pedagogy

On the evening of Thursday, November 3rd, 1994, two sitcoms, *Friends* and *Madman of the People,* playing on the theme of a New York blackout, took the opportunity to introduce new characters to spice up their story lines. In both cases, out of the darkness emerged "Italian stallions," hunks. The male version of the dumb blond has long been the dumb Dago hunk, cartoonish representations of ethnic maleness long part of the popular imagination regarding Italian males. *Wings* has its mostly inept Italian character, Antonio. Blossom's brother on the sitcom carrying the name of the young woman is also a dumb hunk. The "Guido" character is a stable, comfortable and reassuring representation of Italian maleness also used in conjunction with depictions of mafiosi, hoods and rebels to lighten and disarm their impact. Nevertheless, these dumb dagos, innocuous as they may appear, are obnoxious for their tendency to test WASP ways. The test, of course, is always loaded and these poor unsuspecting fools are shown to be less than desirable in stable relationships and meaningful situations.

The cartoonish Italian is akin to other representations of ethnics in popular culture, and though I would not want to suggest that audiences in general may not be able to mediate the effects of media, that option is not always available. Factors that may condition the effectiveness of audience mediation count among them the altered nature of the product when exported (for example, by dubbing or translation) or by the imbalance in availability of information at home. We cannot take for granted that particular readings of cultural products may be self-evident; as an extension of the manipulation of the products, we could also feel comfortable in saying that they are not merely neutral forms of communication and entertainment. In fact, the characters of many such products have come to represent particular registers of thought and ideology.

Antonio Gramsci, if I may be allowed to extract his observations regarding literature and apply them to a contemporary context, defines the function of popular communications media and its influence on the popular.

> When the [personality of the protagonists of popular literature has] entered into the intellectual life of the people, the heroes of popular literature are separated from their "literary" origin and acquire the validity of historical figures . . . The term "historical figure" should not be taken in a literal sense . . . but figuratively in the sense that the fantasy world acquires a particular fabulous concreteness in popular intellectual life. (Gramsci 1975, Q 8 -122)

Though we are all well aware of the role of children's literature, films, and television programming in general in the formation of identity, it was when my young daughter began to want to see some of the same cartoon features that I had seen as a child that that role became even clearer. Pinocchio in particular struck a chord. Not the Collodi book, but the Disney production of the 1950s. When Pinocchio was read to me as a child the first time, I remember it was during a bout with the flu. Mastro Ciliegia and his little Pinocchio, the carabinieri and Mangiafuoco, the cat and the fox, all entered my dreams and became part of the mythology of childhood. Going to see the Disney release of Pinocchio with my father, an exceptional occasion, is an early memory. I can still see the theater entrance with the publicity posters up in the windows. It was winter. And, by coincidence or not, in the large piazza close to the theater someone had thought it opportune to put on display a large specimen of a preserved whale. The film held the attention of all those present, bringing to life the things we had imagined and seen illustrated in the book edition of Pinocchio. But, while all of the characters met our expectations and functioned much in the manner that they did in the book, the brightly colored representations on the screen outshone and substituted the mere line drawings in our minds. Pinocchio became one of those "historical figures" that Gramsci addresses, historical in terms of course different from the clashes of states and nations and their leaders, but historical in the sense of the construction of individual identity within a larger community of children who are exposed to similar things.

Pinocchio and other such books are meant to become enmeshed in the mythology of childhood and youth. All of them go to the formation of a certain type of citizen, who through the reading of these books acquires a certain attitude toward what constitutes truth, community, family, nation, and patriotism. They provide children with a clear-cut reference of good and evil, offer a safe space of belonging and salvation in contrast to the threats of the dark forces of evil and the strange. They offer a space of safe conformism, where it is best to enter accepted norms, to be like others, rather than to stand out . . . to be a little boy like all other good boys. Preferably, all in Technicolor.

Considering the amount of dialogue regarding violence and nudity in film and television, little attention is given to the demeaning and heavily prejudiced characterizations of certain groups, Italians among them. Disney films, sitcoms, and games such as Nintendo's Mario Brothers and the cartoon adventures of the brothers Mario and Luigi (as well as the feature length film SuperMario Brothers), all require us to go beyond some of the purely analytic parameters that dictate the readings of some researchers, who seem to value larger theoretical questions over the apparently banal question of identity. Henry Jenkins and Mary Fuller, in a recent article on Nintendo's Super Mario Brothers, are right to ask questions regarding the lines of "economic and cultural influence" of these works and their "recycling of the myth of the American New World [. . . and its] myths of global conquest and empire building." But their more fearful question of "who is the colonizer and who is the colonist?" (Jenkins & Fuller 1993, 6) regarding many of the products, which are Japanese and thereby unveil American xenophobia, must be undone by redirecting the question toward what myths and representations of others within and outside of itself has America been exporting. How is the diffusion of these re-presentation abroad facilitated even when their currency appears to have waned?

While I don't mean to suggest that the terms of these products always involve considerations of national character or culture, representations of individuals nevertheless come to be signifiers of other nations' characters and cultures. This process of correspondences of course is never as explicit or direct as one might suspect. We must always ask who is being pictured? Who is it that seems to be in control?

Pinocchio is one of those products that finds renewed success through occasional re-release, and one that uncovered for me one of the mechanics of melting pot ideology. Seeing the film in English for the first time, suddenly the characterizations of the competition of good and evil was simplified into a more direct correspondence, in which individuals whose questionable character and habits are directly related to their ethnic persona, to their accented/inflected language. Good and evil are personified ethnically, for in the Italian version I saw as a child the only differentiation was between characters. In the English version the differentiation is between characters as representatives of specific groups, in this case Stromboli's Italian accent and his mannerisms.

Stromboli, who appears to be in control, is in fact a secondary character, and Pinocchio (with the aid of the good fairy) is the one who eventually takes hold of the control that we know was always at his disposal. Stromboli is the externalized other dimension of Pinocchio, he is a figure of antagonism representative of both desires and fears. It is the very desire to be part of Stromboli's troupe, to be like Stromboli the puppeteer (doesn't Pinoch after all want to be on the road, have an easy life with loads of money?), that Pinocchio learns to fear. He wants to be "normal" and not like Stromboli. It is by rebutting his desires and the markers of accent and odd habits (the stereotypical knife play, eating salame) that Pinocchio can hope to conform and assimilate. Pinocchio's yearning for authenticity, to be a real boy, is akin to a yearning for cultural nationalism. Obviously, the training of identity is toward a homogeneous mindset. The effort must be that much more emphatic if the population at large is marked by physical and epidermal differences, and has a recent if not immediate memory of another place and culture. And so, each boy wants to be "normal," each dog wants a collar and a family, each plumber wants to save the beautiful princess and achieve respectability through the act.

Most readers of these products concentrate very intently on all sorts of dimensions, always overlooking one aspect of the work . . . the identity of the characters. And so, Fuller and Jenkins read the Mario Brothers phenomenon purely in terms of exploration and colonization: "Nintendo's Princess Toadstool and the Mario Brothers is a cognate version of that salable, inaccurate, recurrent myth of a captive princess and her rescuers which has been repeatedly read out of, and then written into the mundane records of exploration and colonization . . . When I watch my son playing Nintendo, I watch him play the part of an explorer and a colonist . . . " (1, 4). Mario and Luigi are therefore cast in the clothes of explorers and colonists, not immigrants, not workers, not plumbers, and not read in the obvious and repeatedly expressed stereotyped personae.

But we have the language of the works that the brothers populate. Mario and Luigi are referred to as "pepperoni plumbers" and "eggplant-eating idiots," ("Her Majesty's Sewer Service") and all their expressions are punctuated by

references to food: rotten ravioli, holy lasagna, nervous noo-
dles, perilous pizza, sufferin spumoni, lucky linguini, miser-
able mozzarella. Aside from stressing the one track mind of
Italian-Americans, food is also shown to be the distracting element that often keeps these lazy brothers from doing their
work. In "The Great Gold Coin Rush" Mario wants to take a
pasta break, but is pressed by the Princess to do the job at hand
first. At the very beginning of "Flatbush Koopa," after liberating the mushroom people, the Brothers are in a hurry to go
back to Brooklyn: "Let's go back to mamma's cooking."

This is the "concreteness" achieved by Italian characters
in "popular intellectual life," in the persona of dumb hunk or
chunky plumber. Both marginal and therefore out of the loop
because too easily distracted either by women or food. It is up
to the fairies and the princesses, these representations of sa-
cred femininity that is by no means Italian, to get these men
back on track. In the hands of these women the ethnic characters become instruments for the re-enforcement of the status
quo. Mario's wish to "go back to mamma's cooking" begs the
question where is mamma? Well, the element that has been
missing up to this point, Italian American women, is in fact absent or invisible in much of these narratives.

That "ethnic" women are generally prescribed as less
threatening and more assimilable, and therefore absent in this
type of cultural propaganda, is equally disturbing. Yet I believe
that the reason for their absence is in contradiction to this
sense of lesser threat and greater assimilability. Think of the
potentially disruptive force of an ethnic liberating mamma, of
a matriarchal order of cultural influence.

The products I have briefly mentioned here function to
install in the population at large and children in particular the
notion of the impossibility of ethnic assertion. The men are
constantly called into service by princesses and fairies, thereby
distracting them from their return to the hearth. The disruptive influence of these products on children asserts cultural
difference in qualitative terms and offers seemingly obvious

choices toward homogeneity. The pedagogical turn at this point is one that calls for strategies of opposition that engage both women and men, and a dialogic activism that can make all sides present and influential.

"If I was six feet tall, I would have been Italian"

Spike Lee's Guineas

"**F**ight the Power! Fight the Power! Fight the Powers That Be!" Bensonhurst. Howard Beach. "Fight the Powers That Be!" The place-names signify areas where Italian Americans and African Americans have met in violent conflict. In the media, these are quickly converted to illustrations of ethnic incompatibility and diversity that is posited as a threat to the American Dream. When does America speak of race or ethnicity, if not to re-enforce a negative typology of violent, unpredictable, emotional, and therefore dangerous groups clamoring at the gates of civil society? When do we hear ethnicity mentioned if not during periods of interethnic conflict?

The threat of ethnicity has spawned a comparison with cultism, which represents similarly menacing communities that define themselves (or are defined) as outside of the mainstream. America's relationship to cults being not altogether felicitous, the association of ethnic identity with the end products of Jim Jones' Jonestown, David Koresh's Ranch Apocalypse, as it was dubbed by *U.S.A. News and World Report* or the MOVE "family" feed the fear of difference that seems to run rampant in the U.S.A. As Arthur M. Schlesinger Jr.'s warns in his national bestseller *The Disuniting of America: Reflections on a Multicultural Society* (1993), "a cult of ethnicity has arisen both among non-Anglo whites and among nonwhite minorities to denounce the idea of a melting pot, to challenge the concept of 'one people,' and to protect, promote, and perpetuate separate ethnic and racial communities." Given the generally xenophobic depictions of "ethnics" in the media, this becomes a very appropriate baptism.

While on the surface Howard Beach and Bensonhurst are simplified into white/black conflicts they are, on the contrary, orchestrated beyond the facts to maintain the fictional category of whiteness as an untouched and innocent category. Whiteness is salvaged as the only safe category for all good citizens, no matter what their background. White is in fact a color-blind category; one does not have to be white (as in Caucasian) to be white, for this is an aesthetics, an ideology of cultural absorption and erasure rather than an ethnic category.

The two Spike Lee films that I will consider in the following pages, *Do the Right Thing* (1989) and *Jungle Fever* (1991), might be read to support the apocalyptic warnings of Schlesinger and others who would erase the pluribus from the exalted *E pluribus unum*. However, I would contend that both films illustrate differences between groups in order to highlight similarities that underlines the pluribus in the dictum. Further, Spike Lee's representations of ethnic conflict constitute a critique of white ideology by exposing the mechanisms through which whiteness instrumentalizes ethnic conflict to its benefit.

The undercurrents that flow beneath the violence of Bensonhurst and Howard Beach are related to questions of racial definition, privilege, and inadequacy not only in the relationship between African Americans and Italian Americans, but within the Italian American community itself. Such questions are historically determined in the experience of both groups within the American frame. In order to establish a context for the Italian American component of the equation, I think it might be helpful to briefly outline the historical background of some Italian immigrants to the U.S.A. I will stress here that, though the immigrant experience for Italians might be similar regardless of the region from which they emigrated,

I am most concerned with Southern Italian immigrants for reasons that will be made clear below.

The history of Southern Italy, the region from which most Italian immigrants originate, is steeped in an ambiguous relationship with the rest of the peninsula. Construction of Southerners as the "other" within found support in the research of followers of Cesare Lombroso, such as Enrico Ferri and Alfredo Niceforo, who established the racial inferiority of southern Italians through cranial measurements and other pseudoscientific criteria. The works of these scientists, along with a long-standing myth of the richness and fertility of the land (which such an inferior population could not properly manage) served to substantiate such earlier accusations toward Southerners, ones that justified the annexation of the South in 1861 in what was euphamistically termed "unification."

Much of pre- and post-Risorgimento literature (the period during which Italian nationalism fermented and actualized its desires) illustrates quite well the attitudes regarding Southern Italy. Resistance to unification was painted as *brigantaggio* (banditism), as criminal, in order to veil the repression of a movement that engaged a full two-fifths of the newly established national army, and resulted in 10,000 deaths, and twice as many imprisonments and banishments. The resistance lasted decades, during which typifications of Southerners as Africans, Indians, cannibals, became even more rooted. These assignations were, of course, used in derogatory terms meant to associate Southerners with other equally despised peoples. The rhetoric was meant to justify a military intervention that was then to spread to further colonialist annexations on the African continent; the chronological coincidences between the repression of southern rebellions and the invasion of African lands such as Eritrea are not to be overlooked.

The result of the unification of the Italian peninsula was political and economic oppression which brought about the massive exodus of Southern Italians. During the one hundred years following unification, approximately 25 million Italians emigrated, two-thirds from the south. In addition to this one must account for the additional millions that migrated from the South to the North of Italy to labor in the industries of that region.

The positioning of Southern Italians in a North American, U.S.A., context is problematic, given the slavery paradigm that has fixed a white/black binary system of confrontation. Nevertheless this simple, dichotomous, dominant paradigm has, aside from African Americans, often included other groups deemed racially inferior, such as Southern Italians, Jews, Arabs, Asians, and Native Peoples. F. James Davis, in *Who is Black?: One Nation's Definition* notes that

> in *The Passing of the Great Race* (1916), Madison Grant maintained that the one-drop rule should be applied not only to blacks but also to all other ethnic groups he considered biologically inferior "races," such as Hindus, Asians in general, Jews, Italians, and other Southern and Eastern European peoples. Grant . . . and others succeeded in getting Congress to pass the national origins quota laws of the early 1920s. This racist quota legislation sharply curtailed immigration from everywhere in the world except Northern and Western Europe and the Western Hemisphere, until it was repealed in 1965. Grant and other believers in the racial superiority of their own group . . . consider miscegenation with any "inferior" people to be the ultimate danger to the survival of their own group and have often seen the one-drop rule as a crucial component in their line of defense. (13)

Such a background calls for a deeper investigation into the past relations between Southern Italians and African Americans in order to attempt to understand the distance that has grown between these two communities.

One of the most entertaining ethnic role-playing that involves Italians is that established by Chico Marx in films such as *Animal Crackers* (1930) and *Cocoanuts* (1929). Marx's Ravelli character wears the mask of the Italian immigrant as a vehicle for his Jewish humor, and the mask is often acknowledged in the comedies. Charles Musser's essay, "Ethnicity, Role-playing, and American Film Comedy: From Chinese Laundry Scene to Whoopee (1894-1930)," which treats the Marx brothers' comedies, isolates this ethnic game playing and defines

> Ravelli's choice of a new identity [as] perverse because the guise of an Italian immigrant hardly moves him up society's totem pole to ward WASP respectability. Rather, it is a gesture of solidarity with another "swarthy race." His choice of an Italian persona is a refusal to assimilate. (69)

Similar representations of ethnic shield, or mirror, and solidarity are to be found in many recent films, among which are Spike Lee's *Do the Right Thing* and *Jungle Fever* wherein the mask is often cast as an instrument of various levels of conformism. These films use Italian immigrants as a sounding board to address issues of ethnic inclusion/exclusion, solidarity, difference, and similarity. Lee casts Italians as different, but not so different from Blacks, because in the end they too cannot achieve full acceptance. This re-establishes the Italians' ties with the typifications assigned them in their homeland and as immigrants, and thereby highlights their marginality. The unearthing of these links in the psyche of Italian Americans is most likely the element that instigates the violent reactions toward the visibly different subject that becomes the mirror image of their own oppression.

In the published journal and script of *Do the Right Thing* (1989), Lee writes "that the idea for *Do the Right Thing* arose for me out of the Howard Beach incident. It was 1986, and a

Black man was still being hunted down like a dog" (118). At Howard Beach three African American men were chased from a pizza parlor by a group of Italian Americans. One of the African Americans died as he attempted to escape across a busy throughway. In *Do the Right Thing*, Lee portrays the tensions between Sal, Vito, and Pino, who run a Pizzeria in Bedstuy, and the Black residents of the neighborhood. These tensions build throughout the film until they climax in violence: destruction of the pizzeria, and the death of one of the young African American protagonists at the hands of the police.

But violence is not the central focus of the film. At a subtler level, there is a different type of tension that plays on the similarities between the two groups. Throughout both films, characters take on each other's movements and expressions as part of the process of ethnic masking. Gold chains, hand movements, verbal and physical communication, none are the dominion of one or the other group; Italians act Black, and African Americans act Italian.

Ruthe Carter, costume designer for *Do the Right Thing*, describes one important aspect of ethnic masking or interference.

> When Pino, John Turturro's character, comes to the pizza shop in the beginning of the film, he's all in black . . . Then he changes to a white "guinea" T-shirt for work. When the family closes up shop for the night, John changes back into the black outfit. Which is all meant to support his character's disdain for the work he does and the neighborhood. (7)

Pino's chamaleontic character is indeed reflected in his dress, as are Sal's (his father) and Vito's (his brother). But I would offer that this is also related to the ethnic image that they hold of themselves. All three arrive at the Pizzeria wearing variations of black and white dress, an indication of their socio-ethnic position. Then Sal and Vito wear black tops on the job, while

Pino changes to an all white uniform, apron and "guinea" shirt. Outside of Bedstuy, the black outfit represents Pino's otherness, his blackness in a WASP world, even if only in the safety of his Italian neighborhood.

Within the confines of the black neighborhood that represents society's oppression/repression of blackness, Pino must establish a distance from the situation that will grant him the power that he feels he is denied on the outside. Therefore the "guinea" shirt, because it is white, becomes a sign of power, in the context of the Black neighborhood. Pino likes to flaunt his power either with his younger brother, whom he constantly berates and abuses, with Mookie (Spike Lee), the Black delivery person that works at the Pizzeria, or the Black customers. However, the shirt is the most ambiguous sign of whiteness that Pino could have chosen, since its "guinea" qualifier is one of color difference.

An opposite but parallel figure to Pino is found in the character of Buggin' Out. Buggin' Out is a crucial character in that he attempts to organize a resistance to the Pizzeria's presence in the neighborhood. He complains to Sal that the only photos on the Pizzeria's Wall of Fame are of famous Italian Americans, and that maybe, given the neighborhood and clientele, some famous African Americans should be included.

> Buggin: Hey, Sal! How come there ain't no brothers up on the wall here?
> Sal: You want brothers on the wall? Get your own place, then you do what you wanna do. You can put your brothers, and uncles, and nieces, and nephews, stepfathers, stepmother, whoever you want on the wall, see . . .
> B: . . . Rarely do I see American Italians eatin' in here; I only ever see Black folks. And since we spend much money here, we do have some say.

Sal's refusal fires Buggin' Out to organize a boycott of the pizzeria. However, he finds few allies aside from Radio Raheem,
who irritates Sal with his music, and Smiley, who walks
around the neighborhood selling photos of Malcom X and
Martin Luther King. The confrontation that climaxes the film
is partially instigated by Buggin' Out's activism, as such it presents an important critique of the contradictions of the Italian
American's self-positioning against its historical past, in other
words its wanting to take on the appearance of the dominant.

The part of Buggin' Out is played by the actor Giancarlo
Esposito, who is half Black and half Italian, and early on in
Spike Lee's journal Esposito appears as a potential catalyst for
the film's chemistry, someone to fully represent the blindness
regarding Italian ethnic status.

> Giancarlo Esposito is half Black and half Italian. He
> could play a character called Spaghetti Chitlins (I
> don't know about the name, it's the first thing that
> came into my mind). He's more readily accepted by
> Blacks than Italians . . . I'm gonna have this Black-
> Italian thing down to a T. Some Italians may say it's bi-
> ased, but look at how the Black characters were por-
> trayed in Rocky films. (38)

While not all viewers are privileged to this information, Esposito's invisible Italian American side provides a balance to Pino's character. The name Giancarlo Esposito in the credits
does not provide an immediate link to a black actor. Buggin'
Out's ethnic mask is permanently in place, and he must therefore act accordingly. His alliance must be to the part of his
identity that is most oppressed, since it is to that part that others — like Pino — react. "Rarely do I see any American Italians
eatin' in here" is Buggin' Out's ironical challenge to Pino's refusal to acknowledge his blackness.

Pino is directly challenged regarding his identity by
Mookie in the following exchange:

Pino: How come niggers are so stupid?

Mookie: If you see a nigger kick his ass . . .

M: Pino, who's your favorite basketball player?

P: Magic Johnson.

M: Who's your favorite movie star?

P: Eddie Murphy.

M: And who's your favorite rock star?

(P hesitates.)

M: Prince.

P: The Boss. Bruuuce.

M: Prince.

P: Bruuuce.

M: Pino, all you every say is "nigger this" and "nigger that," and all your favorite people are so-called niggers.

P: Magic, Eddie, Prince, they're not nigger; I mean, they're not black; I mean . . . let me explain myself: they're not really black. They're black, but not really black. They're more than black. It's different.

M: Pino, deep down inside I think you wish you were black. (P laughs.)

M: Laugh if you want to, your hair is kinkier than mine. What does that mean? You know what they say about dark Italians.

The varying degrees of blackness, as they involve Pino and Vito, are illustrated by Vito's association with Mookie and Mookie's confrontational relationship with Pino regarding his identity problems. Vito's interactions with Mookie, his movements, and Mookie's declaration to Buggin' Out that "Vito's down," conflict Pino's assertion of himself within the family, in which Vito represents his Black half, and the community to which he comes every day. Pino's struggle with his duality is beautifully shot by Lee in a scene where Pino in his "guinea" shirt confronts his brother Vito, in black shirt, in the back room of the pizzeria:

P: Vito, I want you to listen to me. I'm your brother. I may smack you around once in a while, boss you around, but I'm still your brother.

V: So what Pino? So fuckin' what?

P: I love you, man.

V: I'm listening.

P: Good, I want you to listen.

V: Jesus Christ, Pino, I'm fuckin' listening.

P: Vito. Black, white . . . No, no, no, no!

V: What the hell you talkin' about?

P: You listening to me?

V: Stop busting my balls. I said I'm listening ten fucking times already.

P: Mookie is not to be trusted. No muligna' can be trusted. The first time you turn your back, boom, a spear right here. *(Pino gestures.)* In the back.

V: How do you know this?

P: I know.

V: How do you know?

P: I know. I read.

V: Give me a break, Pino! I never seen you read nothin' in your fuckin' life.

P: Read your history. It's historical. He, them, are not to be trusted.

V: What you want me to do about it?

P: Be on guard. Mookie has Pop conned already, so we have to look out for him.

V: What are you talkin' about?

P: That's exactly what I'm talkin' about.

The whiteness of the "guinea" shirt fools no one, and is apparently only an attempt at self-deception for Pino himself. "You know what they say about dark Italians," Mookie taunts Pino. This hits the mark directly, not in the sense that Pino wishes he were Black, but that, in fact, Pino's subjectivity (as a Southern Italian) is Black identified. Pino is historically Black.

Finally, in *Do the Right Thing* the issues of identity denial and masking take center stage. In the final scenes, after the pizzeria has been destroyed in the aftermath of the confrontation between Sal, Buggin' Out, and Radio Raheem, and the latter's death at the hands of the police, the crowd turns to the Korean grocery store. The Korean grocer's fate, however, is different; he is spared because he identifies himself as Black. "Me Black, me Black" he yells in desperation. While such associations cannot fully repair racial and ethnic tensions they are elements that have too long been denied by the Italian American community in its urgency to achieve full invisibility within whiteness.

Even Sal, a not unsympathetic Italian American figure in *Do the Right Thing,* maintains his position of denial, a weakness that is most evident just prior to the outburst that destroys his pizzeria. Sal's answer to the events that culminate in the killing of Radio Raheem is "a man's gotta do what a man's gotta do." By washing his hands of the injustice, by allowing the killing to go unchallenged, except by those who might be the next victim, Sal becomes associated with The Power That Be!

Lee's *Jungle Fever* is more explicit in its presentation of Italian racial ambiguity. The representation of the Italian American woman, Angie, played by Annabella Sciorra, could be said to be rather sympathetic. She in fact serves again to make the point as to the proximity of certain physical characteristics that complexly approximate and distance African Americans and Italian Americans.

The film uses relationships between men and women as the central figure around which to discuss issues of race. Paulie Carbone (John Turturro) — *carbone* means coal and therefore signifies blackness — is attracted to Angie, and Ms. Goode, an African American customer. Angie has an affair with Flipper, the African American architect, who is married to a light-skinned African American woman, Drew.

The various cross-over relationships form the background on which Lee addresses the fears of inadequacy of both groups. He uses African American women and Italian American men to explore this fear as it relates to race. The group of Italian American men that gather at Paulie's store find constant irritation in Paulie's interest in Ms. Goode, and express their insecurities regarding their own position as ethnics. Vinnie's feelings for Blacks are made quite obvious by the racist epithets he spews, however, his persona is black in many ways. He is stereotypically Black: he wears many gold chains, he drives a Cadillac (rather than the Camaro associated with Italian Americans), he listens to rap music, and dresses in black, the color he hates. Another character, Frankie, often wears a large gold name plate around his neck, another element stereotypically associated with Blacks. It is Frankie who feels most threatened by the Anglo-Saxon features he believes "Italian American girls" find attractive. As the following exchange illustrates, Frankie becomes enraged when his prowess is put into question as a function of his appearance:

> Frankie sits depressed at the counter in Paulie's News and Soda shop:
> X: What's the matter, Donna got you in a state? I think she's bangin' that big blond headed guy. The one with the big blue eyes, the pretty boy.
> Frankie: What's that supposed to mean? Just because I don't look like that, tall, blond, blue eyes, that don't mean I don't feel like that. What am I, some kind'a Neanderthal? Fuckin' Italian girls, they're all the same. You'd think they'd want their own kind. No. What do they want? Fuckin' Robert Redford they want. Harrison Ford. Who's that other WASP. William Hurt. White Anglo Saxon Pricks. Those bums don't know the first thing about fuckin' romance.

Of course, the irony in Frankie's statements is that Angie is having an affair not with a White-Anglo-Saxon-Prick but with an African American, whose figure directly threatens Italian American desire for waspishness.

When word of Angie and Flipper's affair reaches their families and friends everything explodes and deep seated fears and prejudices emerge from both sides. With the breakdown of their romance, which according to Flipper is an impossibility, given racial differences, Angie brings to his attention that her skin color is darker than that of some "blacks." This both highlights the Italian American woman's otherness in a culture that has fetishised whiteness, and the abuse and rape of Black women at the hands of slave owners that resulted in the wide range of skin color and led to the establishment of rules such as the "one drop" rule to assure continued exclusion of Blacks from representation in society.

As far as Italian American men are concerned, Lee also falls back on the group's worst stereotype: its "penchant for violence and sexist relations with women." Angie's father is ashamed of having a daughter who is a "nigger lover," and in his rage he refers to Flipper as a "black nigger," which would betray his belief that there are variations of nigger among which he might be included; and, toward the film's end, the men at Paulie's shop will physically attack him for his having dared to cross the color line by going to a date with Ms. Goode.

It is perhaps at Paulie's shop that discussions of race relations, social participation and exclusion, and self-hatred are most clearly illustrated. Frankie is offered as the prime focus of self-hatred and racial ambivalence. When he acts worldly regarding the wants of Black women, his mother's identity (and therefore his own) are brought into question; his words once again stress the need to "feel normal," in other words blonde and blue eyed:

In Paulie's shop, the men are asking Paulie about his relationship with Ms. Goode:

Frankie: Paulie. Did you fuck her? You know, colored women, they like to fuck.

Paulie: What?

F: Well, they're built that way. You put a saddle on them, you ride them into the sunset. I'm tellin' you. They love it, they love it.

P: How do you know?

Vinnie: He asked his mother.

F: Hey, what the fuck is that supposed to mean? My mother's not Black, she's just dark. There are dark Italians. Hey, I'm as white as anybody in here.

In the end, these films are nothing if not self-contradictory in their representations. Both racial anger and violence must be recast in the eyes of the viewer, lest we participate in the continuation of the stereotypes as somatic traits. While it is extremely hard to distance one's self from the offensive surface, the "in your face" critique, and to see in it a critique of the group's actions rather than an out-and-out stereotypical dismissal, that is exactly what Lee's films require. The violent Italian American men represent the violence that has continued to emerge in the Italian American community's relationship with its African American counterpart. It is a violence that potentially undoes the family in *Jungle Fever,* and which associates Italian American men with the institutional violence done against women and minorities, it comes to form the mask Italian American wear, one that includes them in the dominant's violent coercive apparatus. They, as other groups selectively designated as ethnic depending on the circumstances, serve to maintain dangerous tensions between minorities, tensions that work to dissipate resistance toward the dominant.

Lee's representations of Italian Americans are problematic in many ways, as are his dealings with issues regarding women, homosexuality, Jews, but it must be repeated that

Spike Lee appears never to speak directly on any matter. The director's convoluted games turn everything on its head. His statement "If I was six feet tall, I would have been Italian," in an interview to Barbara Grizzuti Harrison for *Esquire*, upsets the stereotype of short Italians and tall Africans simultaneously. This is his *modus operandi* to break stereotypes by crosswiring behavior and attitudes.

The character Frankie in *Jungle Fever* finds WASP features more desirable than the blackness with which as "a dark Italian" he is associated. However, as someone so preoccupied with manhood and prowess, Frankie overlooks the stereotypical definition in which he might well revel of black men as "well hung." His desire to be Waspish blinds him to the racism that he expresses toward blacks as a manifestation of self-hatred. I believe that such ambiguities further support my thesis that Italian Americans do not, in these films, merely stand in for whites. Mark A. Reid's recent *Redefining Black Film* (1993), while offering a powerful critique of Lee's films, falls into the rut of dichotomy. Reid sees "the absence of white characters [in *She's Gotta Have It* as preventing] the film from reflecting a radically dualistic world" (94), yet only glosses over that presence in Lee's *Do the Right Thing*.

When Reid does address Lee's use of whites in his films, he quickly points to the "dualistic [nature of the] world." As such, he overlooks other historical/ethnic situations that amplify the scope of the film beyond what many African Americans see as demeaning representations of blacks. Reid criticizes Lee for his "insular portrayal of black life," yet fails to appreciate that the representation of other groups is similarly insular, stereotypical, and "tendentious." We must therefore look into the mechanisms of such overall representations for a more involved analysis of Lee's films. Can we only be insightful regarding representations of our own group?

A simple statement used in recounting the film plot such as "the Italian-American police officers arrive" (102), aside from suggesting that Italian Americans have their own police force, overlooks the hierarchical structure and ethnic competition within police forces in the U.S.A. More than once during the course of the film it is made clear that one of the policemen, the one who ends up choking Radio Raheem, is Irish. This is not an accidental or meaningless presence. The dynamics of ethnicism within law enforcement agencies, which includes blacks, is extremely important in any consideration of ethnic or race relations. For obvious reasons, the make-up of the forces that uphold the law represents a hotbed of ethnic conflict in and of itself.

Finally, while I did not discuss class relations herein, I will only briefly mention that in *Jungle Fever* Lee offers a similar turn-around critique/warning to African Americans. Racism and class prejudice tend to mask each other. By showing Drew, Flipper's wife, in a dialogue with black professional women in which she calls Angie "a low class bitch," Lee forces us to ask if in fact hers is not racism masked by classism. Of course, the question is one that must be asked by each viewer of him or herself. How do we, black and white, men and women, react to the characters in *Jungle Fever,* a professional black man, a black career-woman, and working-class Italians. Is the conflict between the characters in the film a class conflict, an ethnic conflict, a matter of race, or all of these taken together?

Despite the great variety of objections I have heard brought against Lee's films, it would appear that his choice of sparring partners is dictated by a need to provide a space of conscientization and self-education for all ethnic groups as well as for African Americans. This would, in the end, prove profitable for all involved, lest we re-entrench in denial of both ourselves and our histories.

The Intellectual Ghetto

The Italian Canadian writer must write away from the source. What I mean by this very terse statement is that we must not be enshrouded by our past, and nevertheless remain within its gravitational field. It is all part of an apparently contradictory game by which we might retain the past as it is being given up. We must embrace a new culture as it is being rejected, and create an environment where "several languages [are] spoken and several texts produced at the same time." Plurality stating difference is movement and writing. The Italian Canadian, or any other "ethnic" writer, has the task of representing the writer or oral texts of his or her ancestry while also participating in the re-writing of the texts of Canadian literature. We must re-write the contexts of immigrant, minority, and ethnic labels that have been assigned us, and write texts in one and more languages, of which only one may be visible on paper, but whose translations are undeniable shadows of the physical text.

Since immigrants have traveled from one place to another, it is fair to assume that their writing might contain and express a sense of movement. The experience of displacement reveals itself as a plurality of tensions that creates a diversity of definitions in constant motion, toward and away from any readily applicable identity. Writing within this semantic field also establishes a differential relationship to its sources, its multiples, and the very languages of its expression; a movement that both announces and loses itself. I do not mean to imply that we should forget the past; it should be regarded as a dimension of ourselves, and not as what we are.

Writing only in relation the past, in a nostalgic tone or as a simple recounting of it, is doomed to staticity. The passage of time, a future that becomes present, gives life to writing, whereas the non-passage of time, the contemplation of the past, the denial of regeneration and evolution, denies writing the creativity that it seeks. Two clear examples of a constructive use of the past are to be found in St. Augustine's *Confessions* and Petrarch's *Canzoniere*. Both writers use the past as a way of becoming, as movement to make the future present.

I stress these few concepts as basic elements of ethnic writing toward a writing of difference, and not of the different. The writing of the different (ethnic writing) is an instrument by which certain transgressive and liberatory types of cultural expression are kept at bay. To illustrate this I will borrow from the Italian writer and film-maker Pier Paolo Pasolini (a point of origin whose gravitational field extends to include this discussion). The term I borrow is *diverso* (different). The difference between ascribing writing the label of different or difference is quite notable. A writing of difference includes possibilities of development, evolution, influence — the type of writing that holds the potentiality of being a literature useful for cultural activism. Many Italian Canadian immigrant writers however seem to the establishment of themselves merely as different. Difference is stated merely in terms of being different *(diverso)*, with no cultural traits outside of those received or assigned through the history of e/im-migration. If we have concern about being relegated to an intellectual ghetto, a great part of the blame is to be laid at our own feet. A culture of the different lulls us into the belief that we are being left free to express our ethnicity, our history, while in fact we are left free to express only our ethnicity, and that in the terms established by a by-now institutionalized multiculturalism. That sort of assignation is used to limit certain groups' access to, and participation in, the formation of a nation's culture. As it turns out, it is a patronizing attitude that denies freedom of expression and that reveals itself to be simply a case of pure and simple tolerance. The very label of "immigrant" limits cultural influence to the moment of arrival, while giving no recognition to the "emigrant" portion of the equation and its historical and cultural baggage. On the other hand, it is a writing that assures difference as a point of radiation and not of focus. The writing of difference contains not only the various differences in culture, but also the possibility of escape from the "intellectual ghetto" and the delayed action that its influences will have on the official culture.

The English language anthologies of Italian Canadian writing that have appeared up to now have concentrated solely on the writing of the different, of the *diverso*. This is the intellectuall ghetto out of which we must break. We need to break the shell of an ontogeny dispatched to us in order to immerse ourselves in the richness of our differences.

In re-reading this piece it became very obvious that the terms of differentiation that I was hoping to illustrate in the brief time allotted during the roundtable are not as clear as I had hoped. The clarity is obscured that much more by the inherent ambiguity of the terms *different* and *diverso*. Since I approach them in other writings included herein, it will suffice to say here that I conceived *different* as a term applicable to immigrant writing, in other words, writing produced by someone with ties to a culture foreign to the language in which it is done. *Diverso*, on the other hand, I find functional in discussing the work of someone acting from a marginal position within their own official culture (for example, Southern Italians in Italy).

More Than a Thematic Approach

Aside from a few examples, literary criticism in the context of Canadian letters seems to be a suffering animal. We have yet to reach a post-thematic stage, and Italian Canadian writing and criticism is as much conditioned by this type of approach as is any other subdivision of CanLit.

Unfortunately, Italian Canadian writing and other minority literatures make thematic analysis that much more satisfying because they present a new set of themes to identify, describe and catalogue. Though this type of approach may be useful, it is ultimately so superficial that it ultimately limits the potential of the texts it proposes to elucidate. Observations of the thematic sources of texts might ideally lead to a rich substratum of meaning but, alas, the surface is only scratched and insight goes no deeper.

Important questions arise when we enquire as to the function and scope of "literary criticism written by Italian Canadian" and of "criticism written about Italian Canadian work." The criticism written on Italian Canadian writing has mostly concentrated on themes that are assumed to be common not only in specific books or individual authors, but also for the whole of the Italian Canadian community. This approach serves to hide the inadequate background of those who pretend to write literary criticism, and it helps to firmly maintain a stereotypical and easily categorized image of the Italian Canadian writer within the context of Canadian Literature: immigrant is the writer and immigration is the theme.[1]

Since it is difficult to receive adequate critical attention from critics and reviewers, it is probably time for Italian Canadians themselves to take the initiative and produce our own critical groundwork. This trend has in fact already begun with *Contrasts* (Guernica 1986), a collection of essays edited by Joseph Pivato in which we find examples of critical work by Italian Canadians and an enriching variety of viewpoints and approaches.

Alongside critical essays we must also consider the function and effect of book reviews. Few and far in between, it is rather tiresome to read reviews (and not only of Italian Canadian books) that state the same nothingness, that present the same review over and over changing only title and author. It is alarming to find inept reviewers reduced to isolating typographical errors because of their inability to approach a work critically. We cannot be satisfied with superficial readings of our texts. They should be surveyed for the innumberable other selves that they contain. Critics up until now have been blind to these possibilities and have merely been guided by the Italian Canadian label.

What directions would I like to see criticism regarding our work take? Since Italian Canadian writing is deeply concerned with language, it would be interesting and helpful to begin investigations into the importance of the linguistic interaction between Italian and the various Italian dialects, French and English, and the poetic metalanguages arising from the interplay of all of these. The importance of linguistic interaction should be clear, yet it does not seem to be clear in the minds of most writers and critics, whether they be Italian Canadian or not. My own literary work aims to affect changes in English through Italian syntactical construction, and to infuse Italian attitudes into a language to which they are foreign. This type of construct is evident in the work of other Italian Canadian writers, but it is a question as yet to be considered by critics. These textual formations need to be addressed in a formal manner because they will bring to light the sort of relationships we experience toward languages in both the Canadian and Italian cultural contexts.

If others will not or cannot begin to touch the nerves that run through the body of Italian Canadian writing, then it is time for us to expose our nervous systems and explore this fascinating network of meaning. Barbara Johnson has drawn a parallel between the terms *critical* and *difference,* arriving at the equation DIFFERENCE = CRITICAL (Critical Difference). As writings of difference our writing is also critical writing: critical for/of Canadian culture and, by the simply fact of our history, critical of/for Italian culture.

The Failure of Memory in the Language

Re-membering of Italian Canadian Poets

Io speak 'mericano sulamente pe' pazzià.
                                        Pino Daniele

I

The experience of being, and all that it encompasses and touches, seeks expression. Language, a never-ending source of dismay and ambiguity, is one of the tools for such expression and it may take many forms, among which is poetry. The world is much too multifaceted for any one language, and to find an adequate expression for the totality of things in language is an impossibility. Paradoxically there is more than one name or expression for any one particular thing, hence the existence of synonyms. While this situation reveals a multiplication of meaning which increases ambiguity, and reduces the ability to clearly name and define, it also points to a dearth of expressive possibilities. As it turns out, language, our closest ally in writing displays some characteristics that are all but reassuring for anyone seeking to express succinctly a particular experience.

The problem is multiplied if more than one language is brought into play, as in the case with Italian Canadian writers writing either in English or in French. Situations of conflict and ambivalence immediately arise. Use of language does of course bring with it cultural components particular to each specific language, and the act of choosing between languages may indeed be a traumatic one. The relationship one has with

a mother-tongue is as complex and uncertain as the relationship a child develops with its mother. The rapport may be ac-
companied by many similar psychological and physiological
elements. It may be useful to others as well as Italian Canadians to raise questions that will further the study of the unique
set of circumstances that lead to the emergence of non-official
literatures such Italian Canadian writing.

Two interesting writers who have expressed strongly
ambivalent relationships with language are Louis Wolfson and
Antonin Artaud. For Artaud, language and the texts it produces represent a mirror of one's suffering. As he stated in a
letter to Parisot regarding his translation of Lewis Carroll's
"Jabberwocky": "When one digs into the shit of being and language, one's poem must smell bad, and Jabberwocky is a poem
which its author has carefully kept away from the uterine essence of suffering . . . it is the work of a coward, who did not
want to suffer for his work" (Artaud, 185, 189). Artaud objected to Humpty Dumpty's commentary on "Jabberwocky":
"Words mean exactly what I want them to mean; if I want
them to assume more meaning I pay them extra." As a response, Artaud translated the poem by working against Carroll's premise. He devised a work that would do violence to its
original premise and created a poem that was no longer under
the spell of its author, allowing it to speak for itself "according
to its own laws of semantic associaton and alliteration" (Lecercle, 33). This type of relationship with language, one in which
the secure word is taken to be the destroyer of meaning and,
along with it, experience and being, that thrives on uncertainty and the suffering it brings.

In the case of Wolfson, an American of Eastern European
Jewish origin, the rapport with language is similarly one which
brings suffering. His suffering though comes only at the hands
of his mother-language, English. At an early age Wolfson became aware of the intense discomfort that the use of English
brought him. He wrote his autobiography, which describes his
illness and consequent attempts at curing himself through the

study of languages, in French. He refused to speak or write English; nor could he bear to listen to it. One interesting way in which Wolfson developed his studies of languages is relative to his aversion to foods. The English names of foods repulsed him and prevented him from eating. To overcome this effect he devised a game that consisted in finding names of foods in other languages that resembled the English ones, such as the German *milch* for milk. This made it possible for him to drink milk without thinking of it in English (Woflson, 28).

While the important aspect of Wolfson's research and studies lies in his rejection of the mother-language, such a rejection is never total. The word correspondences in foreign languages are in fact instigated and are based on their resemblance to the mother-tongue. Wolfson's complex relationship with English stimulates his exploration of other languages and it does not represent a rejection of it.

II

If we approach Italian Canadian writing with considerations similar to what I have outlined for Artaud and Wolfson, we might be surprised by their applicability. The use of Italian words or phrases by Italian Canadian writers within the framework of poems written in English or French seems so natural as to go unnoticed and without comment. A use that has become increasingly insistent calls for attention through a series of questions: Why use these Italian fragments in poems written in other languages? What is the relationship between the mother-tongue and the other language, between the writer and the mother-tongue? The major reason behind the use of Italian vocabulary appears to be that if functions as a statement of identity, and a way to reclaim a language and a culture that has somehow become distant.

This use of language is by no means singular and isolated. The work of Chicano writer Alurista is an appropriate example of how linguistic and semantic experimentation and hybridization can be used to access identity. However, among the various ways this is orchestrated on the spectrum of linguistic manipulation, so far its use by Italian Canadian writers, while rich in incisive cultural resonance, is apparently only an empty gesture and device.

We have in Proust's *Remembrance of Things Past* a point of reference as an example of the role of memory in the reclaiming of culture. Deleuze has described this process of remembering as one that tends toward a truth. But this does not seem to be a voluntary process. Deleuze states that "we search for truth when we are led to it as a function of a concrete situation; when we [undergo some sort of violation we] are somehow violated and pushed to search for it. Truth betrays itself through involuntary signs"(Deleuze 1967, 18). "Involuntary" is the key word. I use the example of Proust only to correct the thought that he may useful to Italian Canadians. He is not, since he worked within a national language in an attempt to emphasize its historical weight. The truth we seek may not be the one for which we search. Its signs may be brought to the surface by an act of violation, as when two cultures meet. While the clash of cultures may be an involuntary stimulus, the voluntary act of writing and cultural remembrance functions as a balance. In my opinion, much Italian Canadian writing fails to serve itself of the voluntary aspect of the equation. Having accepted the niche assigned to them, Italian Canadian writers mirror a cultural and social not of their construction. How better to express this than to isolate an Italian word among many English or French ones? The locking of Italian words and phrases within a different linguistic environment duplicates one's identity in language and restricts a free movement toward cultural presence.

Elements within language itself deny Italian Canadian efforts at the doubling of identity that they seek. Language can only reflect itself and not any external identity. In fact, the use of Italian vocabulary by Italian Canadian writers creates a context that denies the semantic value of words and serves only to multiply their ambiguity. The relationship I feel would be

more significant, and practical and liberating for Italian Canadians would be an act of will that falls under Nietzsche's definition of truth as an invention behind which lies something
completely different from itself: the play of instincts, im-
pulses, desires, fears, and the will to appropriate.

When we deal with the search for roots and identity of a
Canadian writer of Italian background, we must consider that
for most individuals Italian is a genotypic component and not
a phenotypic characteristic. Italian Canadian writers' use of
Italian is caught within an instinctual search that, as it turns
away from English or French, finds emptiness. The use of Italian therefore becomes an involuntary reaction to this void. A
quick perusal of the writing of Italian Canadians will attest to
this use of language; Italian is not a pretext that may provide
the text with its source of cultural confrontation, but merely
represents a frustrated need to possess Italian. Could the activity of Italian Canadian writers in this instance be considered to
be an act of violence against the mother-tongue? It does indeed seem to create an environment in which the re-
membering, the piecing together of the fragments of culture,
works in contradiction.

III

Another aspect of this particular use of language, which I believe lends credibility to my claims, is that in approaching Italian Canadian texts we are met with an important discovery:
the process of reacquisition is fraught with erroneous use of
vocabulary, grammatical inaccuracies, and cultural stereotyp-
ing. These are elements to be valued within a body of work
that critically challenges officiality. My readings of Italian Canadian poetry in particular lead me to question Italian Canadian writers' relationship to Italian. Their aberrations stand
outside their historical relationship to Italian, their use of Italian is not related to the way in which Italian dialects (or English or French) may have influenced that usage. The results are
parts, "fragments which resist totalization and symbolization,

any attribution to identity or meaning [and] as such endanger the integrity of the subject" (Lecercle, 40). While I do not want to propose the existence of a singular and all encompassing Italian Canadian subject, I do value the multivalent subject that in fact thrives withing the Italian Canadian label. Wolfson himself describes the cure to this problematic as consisting "not in becoming conscious, but in living through words the story of love"(Wolfson, 23), which would assume a multiple presence and not a singular essence engrossed in self-love.

Italian Canadian poets appear to be more concerned with conquering an Italian consciousness rather than in living it through its "words of love." Wolfson's struggle is one that begins with the dismemberment of the mother language and ends with a re-membering of it in a roundabout way. The Italian Canadian struggle is unidirectional, it grows around an attempt at remembering that does not have dismemberment as its starting point. What I mean is that it does not contain an historical consciousness of linguistic choices and usage. It depends on decontextualized fragments and dehistoricized language. While the end point may appear to be the same, there is one important difference: Wolfson's exercise takes him closer to a sense of identity than that of Italian Canadians.

IV

The preceding series of observations could be considered somewhat negative. My critique, however, comes as a result of impatience and the strong belief in the potential of the interaction of languages and cultures. This can be of great value to those elements brought into contrast and to those individuals who partake in it, whether they be writers or readers. The trend now followed by Italian Canadian poets, as far as this aspect of their writing is concerned, distracts from the historical situations that condition their existence and writing. It contradicts their supposed transgression, what Deleuze has isolated in the work of Proust as well, moments in which signs "can also be signs of alteration and disappearance" (Deleuze 167, 22).

Having suggested that the use of Italian by Italian Canadians may in fact signal a loss of that very language, I would now like to concentrate on the effects of this process of loss and the power that such actions yield. The positioning of a foreign word within another language transgresses grammatical rules. The act of undermining meaning (generally grammatical or syntactical) dissolves the function of positing an object. While what takes place is something akin to translation, it is different enough from it to demand its own terms. Transposition from one sign system to another alters the foreign word (Italian) so that, while acquiring a variety of new scattered meanings, it loses its original specific articulation. It implies "the abandonment of a former sign system, the passage to a second via an instinctual intermediary common to the two systems, and the articulation of the new system with its new representability."

In this new representability lies the great potential of a non-official literature such as the Italian Canadian. The system of signification available to these writers contains a greater variety and possibility of exploration and expression due to the interplay of languages and cultures. A foreign word within to the accepted language system defies the status quo and it is set aside and/or overlooked for just such reasons. For these same reasons it can engender "an infinity of new contexts in a manner which is absolutely illimitable" (Derrida 1977, 185). But, I repeat, the activity must be historically grounded.

In the diverse Canadian cultural environment, non-official literatures are not the minority. They hold the potentiality to act upon the official literature, and affect change and evolution. This will be possible through a concept of language that closely parallels Artaud's is expressed by Derrida, who believes that poetic force comes from the wounding of language: "through it, in its opening, experience itself is silently revealed" (Derrida 1978, 80). Such activity however will be hindered by an attitude that seeks to enshrine "non-official" creative endeavors as a monument to immigrants. Italian Canadian literature presents a situation where the wounding is a violence that does not resolve itself. It will remain unresolved as long as Italian Canadians continue to express a false identity, a historical position that has been assigned and not chosen. Italian Canadians must defy their identities as e/immigrants by a critique of those imposed categories. With this awareness we can then begin to properly exercise/exorcise the effects of official and national cultures both Canadian and Italian.

The sense of remembering as a process emerging from dismemberment is related to most Italian immigrants' relationship to language. In order to arrive at Italian as a language of expression, I believe that Italian Canadian writers must first explore their relationship (and the relationship of Italian) to their dialect. By historicizing dialects in the context of emigration and Italian national culture, Italian will be dismembered and offer up fragments to be rearranged by those who are historically marginal to it.

A Non Canon

A canon is a strategic construct by which societies define tradition and outline their interests in cultural terms. Canonical reverence further delineates the distinctions between what is of value to a culture and what is not. It establishes a binary qualitative relationship between the canon and what is excluded from it. It allows control over the texts produced within a society and guides their interpretation. It establishes their value. The acquisition of cultural consciousness on the part of minorities within any national context, and the emergence of a literature that gives them voice, represent a critique of the adequacy of the established canon. In Canada, minority literatures are institutionally supported with the scope of projecting the image of an ethnically rich and diverse society, or what has come to be called the "cultural mosaic." The presence of minority, ethnic, or immigrant writers is tolerated and encouraged, if it fulfills certain thematic prerequisites by which it is easily identifiable as a product of an ethnically challenged person, and which of course unerringly relegates it to the margins of so-called mainstream culture.

While Italian Canadian writing appears to uphold a sense of difference, and therefore opposition to the established canon, this may not always be the way in which it functions. Italian Canadian writers found it useful to group themselves into the Association of Italian Canadian Writers in 1986. The main intention behind the establishment of this association was to be its function as a point of reference in contrast to the dispersed geographical scape. As an alternative community, the group's position must appear united, which entails the structuring of an alternate canon through which to confront the dominant one. Unfortunately, such a homogeneous rendering of the identity of Italian Canadian writers stands on a false platform of transhistoricism that effectively denies the differences within the group. Therefore, paradoxically, by effectively differentiating itself from a mainstream Canadian context and an officially sanctioned minority identity, such a grouping also betrays an idealistic relationship to Italian culture.

The eventual break is not only from Canadian culture but also from the writer's own unofficial Italian history toward an idealized Italian origin. Often, Italian Canadian writers turn their backs on their historical selves and founder in an attempt to recuperate an irrecuperable (because fictitious) past. This fiction has little to offer as a function of the present.

Undoubtedly, the installment of recognizable images and metaphors is fundamental to the establishment of a strong oppositonal canon. The resulting confluence of signifiers goes to instill them as common identificatory markers with which Italian Canadians can supposedly identify. Such a structure marks the rhetorical strategy that, by addressing itself to feelings (of alienation), evokes our most social part and instigates and begs cooperation. However, the danger in such an approach is that often these elements are accepted unequivocally as universally applicable within the Italian Canadian community itself. Therefore, whereas it may seem that these metaphors serve to uphold Italian culture, they in fact mask its diversity through fixing the stereotypes.

At the very level of language, language as metaphor, the use of Italian words within Italian Canadian works stands as an unquestioned commonplace that creates for its users an illusion of belonging. However, this rhetorical use of language denies the linguistic reality of those who find themselves grouped within the emerging minority canon. Does standard Italian adequately express the historical reality of the writers themselves? Is Dôre Michelut's language similar and sympathetic to Filippo Salvatore or Romano Perticarini's? I would venture to say that in fact our common language in North America cannot be Italian, but has to be English (or French, in the case of Quebec). To present Italian as a common language, through which we speak from a community, we repeat the actions of nationalist ideology and further contribute in marking as marginal and inferior our respective languages (dialects).

Alienation is a function of belonging, and those who undertake migration as an internal condition suffer the same problems as those migrant populations who go abroad, even though they do not leave "their" country or "their" language. Thus, while it may language that expresses one's minority status, it does not follow that all members of any one minority are members of the same community, linguistic or otherwise.[1]

How can an Italian Canadian canon be effective if it is only tied to what has been defined retroactively by writers today? In an attempt to canonize themselves, Italian Canadians look back to an ideal Other through which to personify their experiences. However, this idealized immigrant embodies a culture that was never its own, the "national" culture of a pretentiously unified Italy. Writers may in the end be just as guilty of using those immigrant masses to our own ends (by assigning them a particular place in our own teleology) as were those exploitative and repressive forces that imposed on them a "culture" of emigration.

Ironically, the type of canon being constructed for and by some Italian Canadian writers is one that projects itself on an interpretative model that can only hinder its progress, based as it is on predetermined themes and subjects. Current canon-centered writing feeds the narrow view of literary works as primarily nondiscursive forms for rendering accurate representations of experience. They are not indicative of the wide range of Italian Canadian experience in Canada but only serve a self-interested desire for stature and a pursuit of narcissistic self-representation.

Minor poets are major cultural forces, in that their works represent variations on established poetic norms. Italian Canadian writing might aim toward this canonical readaptation of given forms while also forcing writing away from that in which only the themes change according to a particular ethnicity. We cannot accept prescribed positions of ethnicity. Just as Italian Canadians are varied in their backgrounds and cultures, so is their writing a reflection of such variations. We cannot let ourselves sink under the influence of a unified canon such as Multiculturalism and the Canada Council propose.

An unstable, multifaceted approach would better serve us. A non canon would make it impossible to pin down our work through simplistic thematic reviews. The immigrant as subject, that we seem so willing to embrace, does not exist; it is an abstraction that some writers have been trying to live. Now we must rarefy that subject so as to force a reading of our work that is distant from the hitherto romanticized and nostalgic position.

A weak canon, a non canon, finds strength not in an oppositional stance but rather in an ambiguous situation of resistance. Italian Canadian writing (recast in a resistance mode) would concern itself with a critical dissection of tradition (our tradition? their tradition? which tradition?) and not the association of disparate elements through some pseudo-historical affiliation. Part and parcel of this approach must include a critique of origins, not an attempt to return to nationalist notions of culture and language. As a result, exploration and not exploitation would be the tenor, a tactic might emerge through which not to conceal but expose our similarities and differences. The non canon's resistance puts into question all positions of dominant subjects so that there can be no movement toward equivalency. To quote Braudillard: "Defiance, as what always comes from that which has no identity, name, or meaning [the position of immigrants] is a defiance of meaning, power, and truth" (Baudrillard 1983, 70).

An elusive and non-dogmatic approach would be one that better reflects not only our uncertain position as a group but also as individuals in today's world. The difference that must be underlined in Italian Canadian writing is not with Canadian writing in general, but that which is within us. If Canada is to truly become a multicultural society, a society where cultures coexist in a schizophrenic movement free of confines, we must aim away from the establishment of a canon in traditional terms. The replacement of one canon by another to spearhead a confrontation carries with it the colonial attitude we now call a Cultural Mosaic.

What we must examine are the reasons for our writing. Are we concerned more with remembering past notions of what we are (as defined by others who assigned those positions), or are we concerned with discovering what our position may be? For the former, canons play an obvious role in maintaining selective memories of tradition. If we however value the latter, then we cannot but mistrust canons. Once we take a position of disbelief, as we appear to be doing simply by the formation of a group named Italian Canadian Writers Association, then we cannot subscribe to traditional notions of the canon. To paraphrase, and slightly alter, Nietzsche: "As long as there are canons there will be gods." One of our false gods is the "community" of the immigrant that has been assigned us. We cannot speak for a community because there is no community, but we, as diverse representatives of *italianità*, can write to communicate.

It has been said that those who oppose the label Italian Canadian writer, those who do not want to be defined "immigrant writers," do so out of a desire to assimilate into the writing establishment, to conform to the dominant cultural identity. I propose that the opposite would appear to be true. Those who immerse themselves wholeheartedly in the Italian Canadian myth, in the Mosaic fraud, feed the policies of a power structure seeking to maintain a facade of progressive liberalism. The legislation of equality through a filter of preordained ethnic traits and participation in this fraud betray the need to be accepted and kow tow to nationalist notions of culture.

Writing Out of Tongue

There are no innocent languages.

Regis Debray

My mother tongue(s), or rather those that were presented and available to me at the time of my birth, throughout my childhood and to this day, are Italian and Neapolitan. The process of "conditioning" the world, in getting to know, like all children, my most immediate environment, had to be one of translation. All of my contacts with the world were mediated by Italian or Neapolitan.

Later, when my family moved to Canada, English became part of my day-to-day reality. For practical reasons, I had to begin a new series of translations. Whatever linguistic choice one makes, the relationship with the world remains constant. The things I first came to know in Italian remain Italian; those I internalized in English are linked to my English language identity. A banal example of this might be that phone numbers I learned in Italian I can only recount in Italian; those I learn in English I have to recite in English. Even though writing offers the illusion of control through words it involves a series of movements that reduce the distance between words and thoughts, actions, and objects only in appearance. What takes place is a translation that produces superficial graphic renderings.

In our everyday life, we are exposed to various languages (the media, advertising, the language of social contacts, of love and eroticism) which we incorporate without thinking of them as foreign. These movements from language to language are always made in a manner that is actually related to the way we function in our "mother" tongue. It is because of this that I

believe translation to be inherent to our ability to communicate. We are all, in a sense, multilingual and given to
translation.

Here I'd like to introduce the term *atopic* to describe
whatever takes us from our habitual manner of doing, or relating to, things. The word *atopic* comes from the Greek *topos,*
meaning place, and actually refers to the absence of place. I
would further like to extent the term to describe what takes us
away from our habitual manner of relating to things. Poetry
and translation can be regarded as atopic practices that reveal
the possibilities of mutation within language, its "combinatory
spirit." Atopism is a precondition of nomadism. The atopic
subject is unrooted and thrives on multidimensional relationships within his environment. With this design, translation can
be said to be the revisitation of the memory of a missing moment. That which we have not understood or done, that which
is left to do, constitutes the atopic situation. What remains to
be done through re-membering is to arrive at a state in language that is as open as possible at the semantic level. The no-
mad moves through signs that must constantly be
reinterpreted and can never be taken for granted.

Translation is said to constantly represents the transla-
tor's "consciousness of him/herself in the centrality of his/her
own language." However, I would like to suggest that one begins to translate at the moment in which the restrictions of
one's language begin to make themselves felt, when the walls
of language become predictable. When a work finds expansion in another language and not merely in its retelling, it can
be said to have gone a step closer toward its unconditioned nature. Taking the challenge of language through translation
opens up realms of possibility that may not be readily available
through our own primary language. As we condition the
world through language, using it to refer to things, we can, as
Vico professed, only know that which we have made. Our reality is circumscribed by linguistic appropriation. By recognizing this connection we can begin to glimpse the possible.

The acquisition of one or more languages beyond our mother tongue would seem to be redundant. However, this offers the opportunity to re-experience the world in a paradoxical "unconditioned" state. It provides the possibility of viewing objects from a refreshing distance from them to avoid designating and delimiting them.

In my experience, writing and translation are one and the same. I always find myself testing one language against another. But whatever language I use, I am beset at some moment by a lack of words. Writing, as a process of translation, does not recognize any source or target language, but tends to an open ended field of possibilities. It begins in itself and, after a great elliptical trajectory, returns to itself mutated, new, and ready to begin again. Rather than suggest that one is thereby relegated to silence, this phenomenon leads to a state of in-betweenness that is extremely productive and meaningful for writers. With multiple language acquisition one almost nears the elimination of language, in the sense that no one language takes precedence over another.

Since I equated writing and translation, these remarks should be taken to apply to all writing, even that of writers who write out of one language. This condition is the un-grounding of language, grammar, syntax . . . Such is the atopical relationship of migrant writers. Given that each individual that comes to a new language with a culturally different background brings with him a whole array of actions and reactions, this atopic situation is conducive to the propagation of heterogeneity.

This is what the I Novissimi group attempted to do in Italy in the late 1950s early 60s. My own work grows in part out of their experiments with language. I agree with their attempts at a new objectivity, and particularly with Antonio Porta's work, which establishes the decentralized post-industrial subject. However, since the actions of this group were on standard Italian, their linguistic ground soon became a limiting factor.

Another influential writer of the period, Pier Paolo Pasolini recognized this handicap in the work of the Novissimi. He
pinpointed their insistence on standard Italian as the determining factor that would doom their work to eventual staticity. Pasolini defended the usefulness of dialects and other
languages, since he saw them as potentially revolutionary and
diverse instruments of experimentalism. In the context of a
national culture and language dialects are representative of the
atopic.

Writing emerges from the use of language that emphasizes the need for expansion. The expatriate must write
mutely. Writing out of tongue also makes allusion to writing
out of step. To write in someone else's language means a constant readjustment of the forces, both intrinsic and extrinsic,
that lead to action. But it should be clear that by readjustment I
do not mean "to fall in step." The goal is to write tangentially.
The process I am after is one of continuous acculturation, becoming, and diversification. Through this method a number
of disparate elements can be brought together to create a new
environment that is in itself autonomous while remaining re-
spectful of the diverse origins of its components.

Readers are forced to read this work in different ways,
therefore beginning the move toward the other. Terms such as
difference have worked themselves into the vocabulary used to
discuss non-dominant discourses. But their use within the
academy seems to me to be no more than a device propagated
to render lip-service to the marginal and unrepresented. Under the guise of the search for the other, the deconstructing
subject turns back to his own textuality, everything becomes
his mirror. Diversity looks out from the margins to give expression to that which does not originate within the dominant.
From its own sociopolitical and historical situation, it may
participate to some extent in the dominant's view of the
world.

Scanga X Five

Drawing from Memory

When I first met Italo Scanga, and our conversations turned to his interests and influences, the names of Giambattista Vico and Tommaso Campanella emerged. Both these philosophers, in their works *The New Science* and *The City of the Sun,* concern themselves with the world and its making. Their investigations gravitate around the things of the world in order to assess their relationships and their participation in the making of personal and historical memory.

Giambattista Vico's *New Science* reflects on "poetic logic," which is to say, the creative possibilities inherent in language use. Central to Vico's philosophy is the proposal that we can only know what we have constructed, society and language being of primary concern. The philosopher outlines the characteristics of poetic tropes, such as metaphor and metonym, and their development through three stages, which he designated as "divine," "heroic," and "human." Vico's account of the development of language is as follows:

- the divine stage was that of mute ceremonies and rituals;
- the heroic stage was that of gestures and signs;
- and the last, the human stage, was that which marked the emergence of verbal language.

In Campanella's *City of the Sun,* the city's seven concentric walls are used in that utopian culture's educational process. The walls are decorated with drawings, paintings, and diagrams of all the objects and circumstances of the world, including things fabricated by humankind. Children are guided along the walls so that they may learn and reconstruct the memory of their culture, and along with it construct the language of their cultural rapport.

But language is linked to another construct, the nation, the identity of which requires the establishment of a national language, at the cost of any other languages that may fall within its political boundaries. Due to this, an awkward relationship is established between what may be termed official and minor languages. Italo Scanga's cultural origins are Southern Italian, which, in spite of having produced personalities such as Vico, Bruno, Croce, Pirandello, and others, remain, in relation to Italy's dominant culture, part of a minor culture. Southern culture, with its specific linguistic environments, is the culture of a marginalized population that expresses its relationship to the dominant culture mostly through the tropes described by Vico in 1744: metaphor and metonymy, among others. In this context, while one might take Scanga's drawings to be a nostalgic yearning for times past, a nostalgia for either of the first two stages of Vico's schema, I would offer that they are the true *(verum)* representation of silence of the culturally marginal context from which Scanga's work emanates.

The drawings stand for the language of Italy's South, the dialects, the culture that is tied up in those languages, the expression that is silenced and must find an alternative way to refer to itself. Italo Scanga's work becomes a representation of that one condition, of the *verum/factum* (humankind can only know as true that which it has fabricated) of which Vico spoke, that represents not only the depicted landscape or object but the culture and language that has grown from it.

Italo Scanga's work taps into both of these philosophical illustrations. His work reflects both a memory of the past, which he tries to recall and reconstruct, and a memory in progress. The latter is a necessary product of working at a distance from one's culture. Lacking direct access to the past, our future depends on memory, and memory is always a constructed personal language. Fortunately, this personal language speaks of one's ties to culture, in Scanga's case both Southern Italian and American culture.

Viewing Scanga's drawings is like walking along the walls of Campanella's city. From them we, the viewers, learn of the existence of a particular world, a particular vision, and a particular memory that could well be incorporated into our own. After all, Scanga's objects are our objects, only the grammar of their description differs. In this artist's work, we find an invitation to share languages, to reach across that space and communicate through elements of commonality.

Italo Scanga finds in Vico and Campanella vehicles by which he is able to cross cultures to reach from one Vichian stage to another. While he speaks his vernacular language of recollection, Scanga taps into the *vera narratio* of myth/mute to establish its alternative logos geographically, linguistically, culturally, all the while asking any viewer to question his or her own cultural (dis)placement.

Present Memories:
The Photographs of Italo Scanga

Italo Scanga's 1955 photographic series of Lago, his home town, is important to its contemporary viewers for a number of reasons. First and foremost, these photographs are a document of both the life of the artist and of his place of origin. They are a door to the memory of a land and a culture, that of a small Southern Italian town, that has been relegated to the margins of official history. These photographs represent in relationship to dominant Italian culture an invisible culture that reflects a condition of displacement common to that geographical region.

The photographs of Lago are indicative of a way of life that has slowly disappeared, not by its own action but by the encroachment of a paradoxically distant outside world. To paraphrase Roland Barthes, a photograph is always invisible: it is not it that we see, but the objects it re-presents. In Scanga's "Lago Series" there is a doubling of invisibility that renders such a statement even stronger, since the things represented, whether they be a woman, a child, or a landscape, represent an invisible culture. The objects depicted are then merely objects of desire upon which to build a past. Such is the condition of displacement that finds a direct link to Scanga's personal history.

In this series there are photographs of people who have died, of women who married and emigrated to other parts of Italy or to America, of men who left the town out of economic necessity, never to return. We have the products of their labor, artisanship deemed inefficient in today's world. Italo Scanga is closely tied to the people and events in these photographs. They are the elements that culture his life and work. Those familiar with Italo Scanga's sculptures or paintings will no doubt find a familiar echo here. But this is a life past, a life whose fragments the artist has re-collected from a distance to achieve the wonderful mosaic of his artistic production. The very sequence of the photographs, which ends with scenes from a funeral, points not to a nostalgic look back but rather to an appreciative window on a past that is important to all of us. While this past has died, in its death it has given life to new forms and visions.

Animals in Danger

Music . . . there is music coming from . . . what music those animals make!

Upended species . . . feet above the maelstrom . . . but the animal does not let itself . . . does not let itself be read. A part of the sculpture . . . no . . . it's there . . . just itself . . . the only sign of a living thing . . . a living thing. The remains of some living thing . . . of some existence looking upward . . . manifested in the form of animals.

Tribal symbols . . . magic symbols . . . symbols of deferment . . . one or another protector. Distant . . . remaining distant . . . made distant by all that surrounds . . . us them . . . in balance balanced by . . . tools . . . labor . . . sweat . . . imagination.

Their fate . . . not their fate . . . but the overwhelming sense . . . of artistry . . . of inventiveness . . . of self portrait . . . of the construction.

Animals in danger . . . standing where the artist stands . . . on the cutting . . . piercing . . . sawing edge . . . precarious and ecstatic between; animals and geometric figures . . . well measured . . . instruments of measurement . . . instruments of sound. They reside only . . . an odd state of being . . . static . . . held in place ascending . . . a centripetal vector of personality.

Always something . . . beneath their feet . . . in their eyes . . . in our eyes . . . walking a surface opposite . . . projected toward space . . . opposite and unexpected position: the possibility of construction. In place of the artist . . . artists in danger . . . the artist swept off . . . up . . . into . . . off his feet by his creations; a circular movement inherent . . . not the linear drawn . . . not the straight erected . . . the animal artist that springs . . . flows . . . touches . . . begins . . . the animal artist.

Italo Scanga's "A Troubled World"

Italo Scanga was born in Lago, Calabria, where, as a young boy, he frequented the shop of a local furniture maker. It was during that period that he came to know the materials and the type of working space that would later become the main foci of his creative energy.

In interview, Scanga has remarked that the period in which he worked in the wood-shop (World War II) was a time "of survival, not culture. I was energy for [the carpenter]. I turned the lathe, I held things when he needed help. I remember the smells of the shop. I remember him. And I remember the other children helping. He had a beautiful space; you could see far away to the ocean" (Larsen 1984, 71).

From this short biographical note, and the artist's remarks, it is obvious that Scanga has always shown a strong appreciation for environmental spaces, natural elements, and artisanship; these are evident in his sculptures, paintings, and installations. Most of Italo Scanga's work is done in series, all of which comment on some particular socio-political, personal, or environmental event. For example, his "Monte Cassino Series" replays the devastation and anguish felt for that horrendous bombing by the Allied forces in 1944 of the Abbey of Monte Cassino; his Fear series creates a modern man's mythological iconography with wooden sculptures entitled Fear of Buying a House, Fear of Success, and Fear of Money; in the "Potato Famine" suite the artist turns his attention to the 19th century Irish catastrophe, which by extention touches all such problems, not only in his native agriculturally depressed area but, around the world.

The manner in which Scanga acquires the materials for his work supports his close relationship with the world. He collects everything, and uses everything, sooner or later, in one manner or another, or trades it for something else. His constructions are narratives extracted from the world. His tales are the mythos of representation; they are images that give rise to a transformed world, make it visible. Scanga's narrations cut across the face of the everyday toward a truth that coexists with it but lies in its shadows.

A series that further reveals Scanga as an observer and commentator of social conditions is the sculptural series titled "A Troubled World" which warns:

> Danger, diverging interests; Imminent Collapse Ahead; Use with Caution.

Even with such precautionary advice, it must be said that this series should by no means be taken as pessimistic in its view. Indeed, the focus of the sculptures is their "warning sign" nature, one that hopes to open our eyes to man's altering actions toward the Earth. Quite simply, the structures are composed with the following elements: tree trunks, sometimes set on top of constructed wooden bases, from which rise tools such as hoes, rakes, scythes, and long pruning tools. These tools, while paradoxically acting as supports, extend up to impale and cut into metal globes, representations of the Earth. The juxtaposition of wooden trunk bases and metal globes reveals these elements as representatives of different ends of the scale. One is a natural product, the other a metal structure, the product of an industrialized, or at least mechanized, society. While this stale representation of the Earth could be defined as *a-earth,* by extension the wooden trunk itself is something removed from its environment, *un-earthed* as it were.

The juxtaposition of the natural product and one that results from the capitalization of the earth is further reinforced by the tools that hold them together/apart. The globe is cut, or acted upon by the same tools that may have acted upon the tree trunks either by cutting or digging them up. As a result, we must conclude that these tools may be put to a destructive as well as beneficial use. In their essence, they engender the sculptures' "warning sign" dimension. As long as humankind continues to see the Earth as nothing more than something to be exploited for monetary gain, the tools of labor will be the tools of destruction.

The alienatory reduction of the Earth to nothing more than a metal globe, scrap metal, with its multicolored national designations, continues to allude to this destructive pattern. Scanga, by his altering/alternative action upon the globes, seeks an alternative to the pattern of abuse, thus also rescuing the positive aspects of the tools by which we (used to?) live with the Earth. The splitting of the globes by the tools does not serve to release something from their interior, it is a purely an act of force that exposes both the globes' artificiality, as a product of man's manipulation of the world, and the potential violence of such a system. In their connective form, bridging the tree trunks with the globes, the tools take on a metamorphic quality by which they themselves are mutable. They can be regarded as either equal or not-equal signs.

The actions of these tools in an inhuman, impersonal, and shortsighted manner are portrayed by Scanga as taking place mostly on areas of the "developing" world. Those are the areas marked by the words *violence* and *hunger,* ones that suffer the disasters and exploitation, the famines, the environmental destruction, and the economic de- and repression in a post-industrialized world. The deaths by famine in Africa, the destruction of the Amazonic rain-forest, and the flight of millions of peoples from areas where survival, whether economic or otherwise, has become impossible due to the direct involvement of "first" world nations, are signs of global imbalance.

The political designations that would usually crowd the globes, national boundaries, demarcations of possession or belonging, are blurred by Scanga.

In their place, the artist has drawn erratic black lines that seem to mark patterns of anarchic wind movements. Particular countries are totally covered over (usually countries with a strong colonialist and imperialist history), countries representing attitudes that are at the root of the problems commented upon. Again, the words *violence* and *hunger* predominate. Our attention as viewers is therefore drawn to these words and the global problems they engender.

The erasure of national identities, however, should not be misconstrued as a doing away of regional cultures, dialects, and the like for a homogeneous alternative. Scanga is a strong believer in these differentiating aspects, which he recognizes as the truly unifying threads of humankind.

Italo Scanga's Troubled World series clearly evokes elements of hope, represented by the tree trunks and the tools' capacity to change our relationship with the earth, that overrides the series' seemingly negative end. Scanga, as an artist, is not interested in depicting the end of the world, but rather the world's and humankind's potential. Survival is, after all, an art and Scanga, by rescuing pieces of the world in order to comment upon it through his sculptures, makes an art of survival.

Notes from a Troubled World

The world's written skin
its erased surface charts courses
visible only from a distance;
instruments act their supporting wounds.

Fashioned to equal time spent
the work of graphic nullity
backs itself up to an invisible wall;

time is endless
but not the balance
and the world weighs its wound;

the place is constituted by
a constant movement between
blood and sunlight;

there is no hesitation
regarding the addition
or subtraction of elements;

cosmopolitan uprooting of
anarchic winds
a vanguard climatology;

the world
a phantasm
in our house.

Tina Modotti

Toward a Politics of Culture and Displacement

1996 marks the centenary of Tina Modotti's (1896-1942) birth. An immigrant to the U.S.A. from her native Friuli, Modotti lived for a number of years in Mexico, moved through various European regions during the highly explosive decade of the 1930s, and eventually returned to Mexico, where she died in 1942. She stands, in her person and achievement, as an early example of the transgression of conventional political affiliations and the redefinition of identity that necessarily takes place once the confines of nationalism, citizenship, gender roles, and activism are challenged. Modotti's photography and writing served as instruments toward this activity and they developed acutely over her lifetime. Yet, because of other strong personalities with whom she associated, such as Frida Kahlo, Diego Rivera, Edward Weston, and Vittorio Vidali, her work has mostly gone unnoticed or has become enveloped in an aura of nostalgia, romanticism, and mystery that has all but erased its more socially pertinent aspects.

Modotti immigrated to the U.S.A. in 1913, arriving in San Francisco where her previously emigrated father had become an established machinist. Tina began to make a living by working as a seamstress in the overcrowded and overworked production rooms of I. Magnin. Her work as a seamstress in no way precluded her participation in the lively cultural scene of San Francisco's Italian Community. There she acquired an enviable reputation as an able and promising actress in the Community's Theatre Productions. That activity brought her into contact with other artists in the Bay area and led to her meeting the artist Roubaix de L'Abrie Richey (Robo). The couple eventually moved to Los Angeles, where Modotti embarked on a film career, with perhaps the best know of her films being *The Tiger's Coat* (1921). In this and her other films Modotti was always cast as the dark, brooding, and sensually dangerous Italian or Latin woman. Her appearance in film was symptomatic of the sort of casting that might be expected for the period, and it is most likely that these representations helped propagate some of the femme-fatale aura that surrounds her figure to this day. Robo's sojourn in Mexico, with his eventual death there, caused Modotti to also travel south. While her first trip was to briefly take care of Robo's funereal arrangements she subsequently returned, attracted by Mexico's active art scene.

Eventually, at her insistence, Edward Weston, whom Modotti had met through her contact with the bohemian artist groups she had come to frequent in Los Angeles, joined Modotti in Mexico. There her home soon became a gathering place for artists, writers, and political activists, and it is during this period that the names of Frida Kahlo and Diego Rivera became forever associated with Tina Modotti's.

In Mexico, Modotti began to practice the art of photography to augment her political activism. Her association with Rivera and other Mexican muralists fed a cultural/political aesthetics and ideology that became her all-consuming passion. Her activism and her strong criticism of the Mexican government made her a target of governmental investigations and harassment. All this culminated in 1929 with the assassination of her Cuban lover, the political exile Julio Mella. Modotti was accused by the authorities of having participated in the assassination; she was brought to trial but was eventually acquitted. Nevertheless, this episode in association with other previous incidents, and the additional accusation of having participated in the plot to assassinate then-president Pascual Ortiz Rubio, led to her expulsion from Mexico in 1930. At that point she returned to Europe where, under the watchful eye of Mussolini's Fascists, who sought to re-patriate her to Italy in order to try her for her anti-Fascist activities, she traveled to Berlin, the Soviet Union, Paris, and eventually to Spain as a participant in the Civil War. In 1939, after having been denied re-entry to the U.S.A., she clandestinely returned to Mexico, where she died three years later under what some consider to be mysterious circumstances.

Modotti's work as artist, writer, and activist forms an important part of the cultural legacy of the early part of this century, a period during which much of the nomadism and transculturalism that define our contemporary society began to take shape. Long pigeon-holed as a pupil and protégé of Edward Weston, Modotti's body of work suffered from such labels and she was relegated to the secondary ranks of art history until recently. It was most likely her friendship with Edward Weston that influenced Modotti in her choice of photography as a tool of expression. Nevertheless, we cannot discount the influence that her uncle's photo studio in Italy, or her own father's commercial photographic career in San Franciso, might have had.

While Weston created a niche for himself between the pictoralist, documentarist, and avantgarde photographic movements of his time, Modotti's sensibilities and interests drew her closer to street photography and the documentation of popular lifestyles and customs. As it has become apparent, the use to which Modotti was to extend photography was uniquely hers and influenced in part both by her background and her ideology. Having grown up for part of her life in the Friuli, an underdeveloped agricultural region, she would have had a rather direct contact with the hard life of its inhabitants. This undoubtedly led to her identification of Mexican urban poor and rural populations as part of a global class of marginalized peoples and cultures.

Definitely touched by a sense of aesthetics that is almost classical in its composition, Modotti's photographic work is nevertheless a statement of protest against the social conditions of the time not only in Mexico but around the globe. If to "show poverty and injustice is to protest against it," as Italian neo-realists were to state in post World War II Italy, then Modotti's photographs form part of a cultural legacy that still holds an important place in political history and activism, as well as in art history.

While "realist" or documentary photography that depicted the "suffering masses" is said to have begun with photographers such as Lewis Hine in and around 1935, Tina Modotti had been hard at work producing exactly that sort of socially relevant photography already for almost a decade. What distinguishes her work from that of documentarists is that her subjects are directly representative of historical and political events, be it the failures of the Mexican Revolution, or the struggle against Fascism.

It must be pointed out that Modotti's interest in this class is reminiscent of the Italian Marxist Antonio Gramsci, whose writings on folklore are in general traceable to the mid-1920s. In contradiction to the accepted myths regarding the peasant classes and their beliefs, their folklore, Modotti and Gramsci apparently shared a view of "folklore as a concept of the world and life . . . distinct from official concepts of the world" and stated their belief that "only in folklore does one find the mutilated and contaminated documents" of history that make folklore kinetic (Gramsci 1991, 6). It is exactly this kinetic energy of culture that radicalizes folklore and all its associated beliefs in myth, magic, the supernatural and the natural world, and identifies within it its revolutionary potential.

The use of photography to engage folkloric subjects and products, and as such to represent what is in fact a divergent sense of technology, might seem contradictory. However, Modotti's art acts in the appropriation of photography to offset its uses as a technology of cultural determinism, as is the case of its use by ethnographers and anthropologists in service of imperialistic or colonial enterprises. The works of photographers such as Wilhelm von Gloeden, in a less obvious way, and of J. W. Lindt, in a more overt manner, defined a hierarchy in both racial and cultural terms through their studies of "indigenous peoples." Modotti, on the other hand, used photography as a manner of expressedly manifesting undeniable human and cultural presences as equally valuable alternatives to officially recognized ones.

However, Tina Modotti's time behind the camera was short. During her life of forty-six years, Modotti dedicated approximately seven years to photography, and about fifteen to political activism. Her interests in these two fields are not so chronologically well-defined; there was, in fact, a very obvious overlap of interests and activities. Modotti's photography cannot by any means be considered a purely aesthetic exercise but, as both her photographic subject matter and her writings reveal, it is a rather close interweaving of ethical and aesthetical attitudes.

As such, maybe too much has been made of the fact that Modotti gave up photography during her residence in the Soviet Union, and for the rest of what remained of her life. Photography had also been, for the nomadic Modotti, a means of culturally constructing herself. Viewing, capturing on film, and ideologically assessing her subjects, was a way for Modotti to emphasize her own presence/absence in Mexico, and the absence/presence of a precise cultural context of her own. Many different reasons have been given for her abandonment of photography, enough to propagate the already swirling mythology that surrounds her. The list of reasons ranges from the dramatic, her having thrown her camera into the Rhine as a declaration of political activism vs. art, to her inability to produce photographs for political papers, to her supposed incapacity on the technical level (the use of a Leica 35 mm format rather than her usual large format view camera). Topping the list, among those blamed for having caused her to dismiss photography as a viable political tool, is the Italian communist Vittorio Vidali. He is assigned the bad-guy status for having insisted that Tina dedicate her life to political activism. Any one of these versions unjustly undermines and underestimates Modotti's own ability and character, as well as her commitment to the causes she chose to support.

The questions that must be posed with regard to Modotti go to the issues that feed her art and ideology, and that in return reflect that art and ideology to form a holistic sense of being-in-the-world. Uppermost among these must be the influence of her status as a double emigrant and her subsequent nomadicism. We have, in her work, a site of specific discourse that reveals aspects of her particular views on personal identity as a product of engaged hybridity, that is to say: a foregrounding of hybrid influences in all their variations and the engagement of those toward a definition of self.   .

Repeatedly hailed and acknowledged as a singularly important figure and influence in contemporary Mexican photography, Modotti was not Mexican. Sought by Mussolini's Fascists under accusation of crimes against the Italian state, she had left Italy as a teenager never to set foot on Italian soil again. As an important American artist and activist she was designated persona non grata and refused entry into the U.S.A. on her return from Europe following the Spanish Civil war. This list of non-definitions and exclusions according to nationalist designations should make clear that identity is an amorphous concept, hardly sustainable by notions of citizenship. Rather, as Chantal Mouffe has expressed it, "by resisting the ever-present temptation to construct identity in terms of exclusion, and recognizing that identities comprise a multiplicity of elements, and that they are dependent and interdependent, we can 'convert an antagonism of identity into the agonism of difference' and thus stop the potential for violence that exists in every construction of 'us and them'" (Mouffe 1994, 111).

Modotti appears to have been predisposed to activities that led her to an (e)valuation of alternatives, the sense of "agonism of difference," and less interested in the otherwise more common political need to antagonize along dichotomies of position.

She showed remarkable insight into the limits and contradictions of Marxism itself, especially in the relationships between the peasant, the proletarian, and the subproletarian classes. Through her photography Modotti raises into prominent view not only the social by-products of capitalism, its influence on the working class and socially marginal groups, but she most definitely gives prominence to the bodies and activities of subproletarians and peasants (in Mexico this means a class that suffers great exclusion at all levels of society and which includes the indigenous peoples, or Indian populations). It is through this representation of a hardly considered reality within the Mexican social landscape that Modotti forges that hybridity of concerns that undermines "us and them" paradigms and defines a social space by shifting the focus of oppressive forces by presenting a potential series of alliances active within the field of hegemony. Her photographs are a manner by which to redistribute explanatory power; they establish the coordinates not only for photography as a viable social practice, but for the position of the subjects portrayed within it.

Influenced by her disinterest in nationalisms and their congruent identities, and her own obvious experience of migration, Modotti's photography is strongly marked by her interest in hybridity. While not necessarily creating or defining hybridity, she seeks out subjects that personify it. Hybridity is a dimension that is not defined from within but is exercised from without: without power, without citizenship, without privilege, without voice. And, in Modotti's photographs, it is the subject matter, what she values culturally, socially, ideologically, that lends hybridity to her exercise. "By accepting that only hybridity creates us as separate entities, it affirms and upholds the nomadic character of every identity" (111).

Hybridity as a concept requires that it be defined for every exercise in which we bring up the term. At first it may seem an odd concept to couple to photography outside of the purely technical realm, because supposedly there is only the act of taking a photograph, something that Modotti herself thought to be a purely objective exercise (though we know otherwise both in general terms and for Modotti's own practice). If there is no manipulation of the image where does the hybridity begin to manifest itself? And is it part of the artist or of the product? With Modotti's early work, and let us remember that she apparently produced less than 300 images over a period of about eight-ten years, it could be said that it is apolitical, purely aesthetical in preoccupation, and merely a reflection of Weston's influence. But it may be in those very still-life exercises of her early period that we might find the clue to lead us closer to Modotti and her work. Still life means literally to emphasize that the subject matter is alive, culturally or otherwise. Ideologies are ideologies and just that; humanity is on the other hand a whole other matter, and human subjects are still lives in the sense of living. It is at that point that hybridity forms, in the meeting of the photographer and her subject matter both through the camera lens and outside of it.

The early still lives were training for her human photography. Differently than for some other photographers, Modotti was able to befriend her subjects and the photographs show exactly that: there is no timidity and no reluctance on the part of her subjects to be photographed. It is this hybridity that forms what Rivera pointed out about Modotti's work: that it is a truth that is pedagogically powerful for its immediacy, for its particularly strong support of revolutionary ideals, even if she eventually became quite disillusioned by the beauracratic aspects of the communist hierarchy.

It is this confident consciousness that makes of Modotti a figure of great importance for she very smoothly, so smoothly that we may miss it, brings together as tightly functioning and inseparable, aesthetics and ethics. Does it diminish her significance if she writes on the back of a photograph something completely and utterly mundane? No, unless we forget that the photographer too is also a living entity.

Read as such, Modotti's photography reclaims its stature as a political and ideological product and critique, greatly distant from the commodification it has undergone within the art market where, over a period of only a few years, the value of her work skyrocketed, to bring in 1989 one of the highest auction purchase prices in photographic history. Much of the work done on Modotti has been from an art history perspective, which as well as providing a cultural/historical context for the work, also functions to stoke the fires of the art market machine. Tina Modotti's value today is still primarily the value attached to her photos by the market, which is greatly boosted by the very limited number of vintage prints available. That value must be clarified and enhanced beyond this dimension, not only to recontextualize her art, but also to expose the nullifying and neutralizing effects of the market on the sociocultural and political value of her work.

Art historians have almost exclusively concentrated on the relationship between Edward Weston and Tina Modotti to revisit the concepts of originality and influence, for these are the elements by which hierarchies within disciplines is defined. Thus, Modotti's history has been outlined in the shadow of this great photographer and has suffered for it. The market does not recognize the confluence of political, cultural, and other forces that go to inform the photographs it commodifies, it thrives on terms of authenticity and originality that it establishes for its own benefit, terms that are, in the end, in full contradiction of Modotti's philosophy.

A Poet in a Moving Landscape

An interview by Dino Minni

Dino Minni: *You lived on Vancouver Island for some years and felt isolated there. Was the isolation geographical or cultural?*

Pasquale Verdicchio: Maybe a little bit of both. The geographical isolation I liked. I enjoy islands, probably only because of the water that surrounds them. And Victoria, if one can avoid its sometimes Disneylandish facade, is beautiful. I like almost any place if I can leave it behind for a while every now and then. Culturally, Victoria is probably no different than Vancouver, except that it's smaller. It tries very hard, and there are communities of writers and visual artists there that produce quite good work. Unfortunately some of them never leave the island — I don't mean physically — and get bogged down . . . doing copies of copies of copies. Then there was the "West Coast Renaissance" that was announced in the *Malahat Review* a few years back. I don't think that ever went anywhere. A Renaissance needs more than incestuous metaphors. Like any other definition that comes before any real movement is at hand, the "West Coast Renaissance" failed in that it tried to build on a few writers and spawned little new material. There was no philosophy behind that "movement," and I am convinced that in order to produce a lasting literature one has to build upon some sort of philosophy.

A Renaissance should give new material the possibility to develop, not proliferate copies of old material. I also believe that "West Coast" is too wide a term: Vancouver writing differs from Victoria writing, and so on up and down the coast. Maybe the "West Coast Renaissance" was trying to identify itself in too small a number of artists.

You've traveled. Has this expanded your literary horizons? Has traveling made you more cosmopolitan in outlook?

I don't know if it has made my outlook more cosmopolitan. I think either you start out with that sort of outlook or you don't. As far as expanding my literary horizons, that is again an instinctual thing, to read other literatures or not, it's something that develops from need and curiosity. Traveling may help in recreating a certain environment that is missed due to our ignorance of other cultures: reading *Zorba the Greek* or *The Odyssey* in Greece, or Garcia Lorca in Spain, or Cesare Pavese in Italy. But, again, traveling is not necessary to bring one to foreign literatures or to find an affinity in other writings. What travel does for me is to fulfill another need, one very closely related to the need that writing attempts to fill: to find yourself somewhere, on a beach, on a hill, on a street, or a page, and feel somehow relaxed, removed and belonging. Travel has also given me the chance to meet writers from other countries, something that can only help in increasing political, social, and cultural awareness.

At the Rome conference [on Italian Canadian culture] in May, 1984, you came in contact with many other writers of Italian Canadian background. Was this an important happening for you? In what way?

Yes, it was extremely important for me and, I believe, for everyone else there. It was the first time that so many of us had been together in one place. It worked in giving a sense of community, especially since it was in a land that marks some sort of a beginning for us. It also put clearly on display our differences, our philosophies, our politics. I felt a great attraction to the group from Quebec. Their intellectual background is closer to mine, probably because of the cultural connections between Quebec and Europe. I think, though, that we failed to come to grips with one thing, and that is our place in the overall scene of Canadian writing. Joe Pivato did say something to the effect that we were in a transition state between immigrant writing and something else, and Amprimoz expressed his belief that some non Italian Canadians had been influenced by Di Cicco's work. But these are things that are yet to be studied. We need to reassess our writing. Do we want to keep writing about immigration? The recent anthology, *Italian Canadian Voices* (1984) seems to answer such a question in the affirmative. There is very little in it to convince an outside observer that we, who write with the label *Italo-Canadian* over our heads, are able to approach any other subject. The section entitled "Presence: Poetry 1979-1983" represents the writers of Chapter II of the same book (which is a republication of sections from *Roman Candles*). What has happened in the six years between *Roman Candles* and *Italian Canadian Voices?* Apparently, nothing. Where is the transition? To what? Where is the new poetry? There is a new poetry out there, written by Canadian writers of Italian background, but part of the disregard toward it is due to the fact that it does not serve the purpose of multiculturalism.

Another area in which we suffer is criticism. Paraphrase is not criticism and it does not fulfill criticism's aims: to act as a catalyst and stimulus for change and evolution. We are in need of critical thinkers all across the board in Canada.

At this conference you showed your dislike for the label Italo-Canadian writing. Explain.

As with the label *West Coast Renaissance,* this label that has been attached to our writing does us a great disservice. It does nothing but restrict our writing. To be a "real" West Coast writer it seems that one has to restrict one's self to the West Coast canon, the accepted series of metaphors: bones, feathers, stones and algae. Similarly, an Italo-Canadian writer has to follow that particular canon: write about your mother in her mourning clothes, your father laying bricks, your first trip back to Italy. No! That only works for some. We did not all have the same experiences, therefore it cannot be a "stage" applicable to all those who write and happen to be of Italian background. The problem is that if one does not ascribe to the canon he is disregarded by both the "official" and "minority" literatures. That writing will get you into the Italo-Canadian anthologies, but it may keep you there. It's a trap from which few can escape. Once I asked Di Cicco in an interview if he felt himself to be a spokesperson for the Italian community, what he thought of his being labeled an Italo-Canadian writer. My answer is the same as his: "My only allegiance is to language." You see, a label like Italo-Canadian presupposes a position, it hands you a neat little package of poetics and does not allow room for a personal one. It is nothing more than something that has been given us from the outside, not of our own choice. Pasolini talks of this type of thing in terms of an "intellectual ghetto." Yes, we are allowed to write in our own predetermined way, our own little Italo-Canadian material, but don't step out too far. It's a way of keeping people at bay, such writing betrays a "tolerant" attitude on "their" part, but not one that will go further, into full acceptance. Any writing carrying a label like ours is doomed to remain entrenched in that label. A writing without predescribed limits is one that will flourish, anything else is doomed.

The last time we talked you mentioned that you have deliberately avoided the theme of immigration in your poetry. At the same time you confided to have shared the same feelings of duality and ambivalence as the rest of us. Would you elaborate?

I don't think I deliberately avoid the theme of immigration. I've never really felt an immigrant. I've felt alienated, and yes, a feeling of duality or multiplicity. But such feelings are a natural result of being in some way different; one does not have to be an immigrant to feel like that. There is a state of mind that could be labeled "immigrant" even if one has never emigrated. Even though I don't talk directly about immigration, I am sure that it comes through in my work. I don't think it can be helped. It's not unlike any other writer who moves through language. To write is to migrate, to be in constant movement. Language is not a sure bet in one's search for identity. Language is an attempt on the part of man to control what is around him, and as such is a reflection of his paranoid and schizophrenic character. Every person who picks up a pen leaves himself open to ambiguity.

The central question in Italian Canadian writing is: Who am I?, which mimics one of the three questions of all Literature (with a capital "L"): Where did we come from? Who are we? Where are we going? In Moving Landscape *there is no identity crisis, no search for roots?*

Oh, certainly! Both are present. But, as you stated in your question, these are basic problems faced by any writer. I don't see them as posing different problems for "ethnic" writers; such writers are working out the same problems as anyone else. There are two points here: 1) you give the ethnic writer extra credit and value his writing more because he is doubly perplexed and better illustrates a writer's plight, or 2) you value the ethnic writer less because he is stuck in a mode not of his own choice in which he is unable to express himself fully, and which acts only as a prison. I don't agree with either one of these propositions. What I find particularly disturbing is the conclusion to an article that I recently read, which stated that Italian Canadian writers would not be writers if they did not have their immigrant experience to draw on. I'm afraid that anthologies and writing tailored to suit a particular ethnic image proliferate this type of conclusion, and are dangerous in that they constitute auto-limitations. My identity crisis, my search for roots takes place in language. I don't write to find out if am really Italian or Canadian, or to express my anguish at having to leave my native land. I write to question.

There is however a search of a different sense. In fact, Quill and Quire *in "New and Forthcoming Books" describes your collection "as the world seen through the eyes of an explorer." Travel and discovery are recurrent themes. In this sense, you are an immigrant?*

Yes, as all writers are migratory. We set out on a voyage across the page, across language not knowing what we'll find, or if there will be a return. If there is a return, to what do we return? Language. So we're lost in a labyrinth, and the fun is in trying all the paths and forks in the road.

Or am I on the wrong track? For all poetry is discovery — that is, seeing the ordinary with a fresh eye.

No, you're on the right track about poetry being discovery, but more than a fresh eye, it's the want and need to look beyond the surface of things, through the folds of reality: a willingness to leave port without a map and travel by the stars.

Reality and illusion are also explored in your poetry. I'm thinking of such poems as "Ancestors," "Woman at the Well," and "Moving Landscape." Would you comment?

The problem is in knowing where one leaves and the other picks up, and I am not aware of any particular signs that may aid us in reaching a conclusion in that regard. So, I'm convinced that our job is not to interpret reality, but to misinterpret it. To interpret is too definite, too sure of itself. Every poem is an attempt, a potential interpretation, but most likely a misinterpretation. The reality of Italian Canadian writing is one of the things we should be reassessing. As I said before: I write to question. I question the "real" and "reality" that is assigned to us. I don't want to be told that my reality is an "immigrant experience." Who has created that reality for us? Why? How can anyone be so sure of what it is to be an Italian Canadian writer? The woman in the well poem does not care as to which is the reality. She accepts the well as one reality; whether real or not it does not matter. Who is to say what is illusion and what is reality? We live a reality that for our ancestors was an illusion. What happens when we say we have become disillusioned with reality? See, there's language with its tricks. Illusion is not reality, but what is disillusionment with reality? Language, that's what we have. What we write on a piece of paper is . . . ? Well, I believe that's where we should remove ourselves from our assigned reality and see our "function as an absence." We are removed from it and we are part of it, but I'd hate to name it one way or another.

The word dream *is a favorite.*

Are dreams illusions? I have always been fascinated by the thought that dreams could be our reality. I dream of realities. Therefore I dream illusions because dreams can't be realities. Or is it the other way around? What I am getting at is the total lack of certainty, the ambiguity in which we live and constantly deny.

Other words are moon, fish, water, wind, and fossil. Can we detect a West Coast influence in the use of these words?

All natural elements. All connected. The moon affects the movement of tide waters; the movement of body fluids. Wind is the interspace between earth and moon. Fossils are the ancestral animals and plants. They are symbols that contain signs. They represent themselves and other systems of signification that I can only attempt to understand by juxtaposing them. A fossil is a message. The wind carries messages. The moon has messages in the form of craters and canals on its surface. Water carries sound faster than air. Fish move their lips in a seemingly silent language. As to the possible West Coast influence that these words may betray, yes, why not? I could also answer:

Which west coast? Naples is on the west coast of Italy, and the sea and fish have always played a part in the formation of my intellectual touchstones. In such correspondences may lie the secret for us, and that is where we should try to work. The editors of *Canadian Literature,* for their special issue "Italian-Canadian Connections" (No. 106), chose two of my poems that clearly display this link. Both include the word *cactus:* one on the island of Formentera, the other in the interior of B.C. We exist in the interspace of these distant foci.

You're bilingual. How does this influence your poetry?

I'm convinced that it is possible to write Italian poetry in English and English poetry in Italian. Mix up the syntax, overlap meanings, and other such things. Having more than one language to work from increases one's possibilities. I write in both languages, they can work with each other or separately. I'd like even more languages. Of course one influence would be found in the reading of poetry from both languages. Again, it opens up new doors. It's different from reading things in translation. Often translations cannot convey nuances. I am not against translation — as I have already said, it makes up an important part of my work — but if one can read something in its original language, so much the better.

Scattered Verses Between Naples and Canada

An Interview by Sergio De Santis

A forced existence of nomadism detaches a man from his center, creates a space that calls to be filled. In the best of cases, this space is fulfilled by inventions and words that can become poetry, as it has for Pasquale Verdicchio, among the most interesting Canadian poets.

His collection, *Nomadic Trajectory,* reveals the choice of having compensated for nomadism by making literature his territory, his residence.

Verdicchio's roots sink so deep into the culture of his place of origin that he could easily be characterized as an Italian poet writing in English. His writing recalls in some instances the work of Antonio Porta, and *Nomadic Trajectory* actually begins with a quote from the Milanese poet of the neo-avant garde. His deep voice at the other end of the phone seems to betray the unrest of someone who knows, as Adorno writes in *Minima Moralia,* that "in the end a writer cannot even inhabit language."

In Nomadic Trajectory there is a poem, "Parthenope," in which Naples is identified by its longitudinal and latitudinal coordinates, almost as if the reference were solely to a geographical place.

The coordinates serve to define in an artificial manner a place that is what I in effect consider my home. For me it represents a steady place. Even if almost thirty years have gone by since my emigration, I still live in a sense in via Bernini, Naples. It is no longer so, but it still feels that way. It is a place of memory that can be defined at least with geographical coordinates.

Still in "Parthenope," there is a reference to the "negated city."

Yes, the city is negated/denied but from outside rather than by Neapolitans themselves. Denied in the sense that there has been a forgetfulness on the part of History. Every year I try to come back for a little while. In June of this year I was there for a couple of weeks. Every time the problems seem to multiply and worsen. However, I find the city is always teeming with life and activity. This activity and movement is what I try to represent in my poetry.

In your work, blank spaces act as intervals between words. What is their function? Are they representative of things left unsaid or a stylistic pause?

Yes, they are unsaid words that leave space for the reader. They are like the alleys of Naples, in the way that they are suddenly interrupted and then continue, then are lost and found again through other streets. The blank spaces are there so that a reader may stroll inside the verses, and to offer a reflexive pause regarding what has been said and what may come.

In "Parthenope" Naples is also defined as a "necropolis." However, earlier you stated that you found the city to be vital.

I perceive Naples as a city of the dead, always taking into consideration that Neapolitan culture, and southern culture in general, is buried beneath the common place and folklorizations. I don't intend a necropolis as a place of static death but, rather, as a place of constant mutations not always recorded by History.

One of your verses refers to "one city yet all possible cities in fragments."

For me Naples reflects all cities, the world, even if some would suggest that it only represents the decadence of the modern world. In that restricted sense, if one goes to a place like New York it is obvious that there are cities much worse off than Naples.

You refer to yourself as a traveler between worlds. What insights has this nomadic perspective given you?

That culture is a matter of subtraction, of absence. Culture is not that which one has when leaving a place, but defined by that which is lost along the way.

By leaving the place in which one has roots something is lost?

First from Naples to Vancouver, then to other Canadian cities, then back to Italy, and finally to Los Angeles and for now San Diego. My distance is multiple, from my language, from my roots, from myself, from everything.

Is this the reason for the title of one series of poems, "A Critical Geography" [now in Approaches to Absence *]?*

Geography is for me a dimension in constant movement. It has traversed my life and has left its mark on my body, my language, my mind. I intend here a Neapolitan and meridional geography, rather than Canadian. There are some reviews of my work that refer to an American tradition. However, I don't recognize myself in this tradition and I barely know it. I have always looked to Italian poetry, and I feel an affinity to the new generation of Italian poets. Many of the courses I offer in the Literature Department at the University of California, San Diego, emphasize meridional culture, and I also teach a course on Italian expatriate culture. In addition, I am completing a book regarding these same subjects, re-reading history, the place and function of southern Italians abroad, in other cultures.

How did you come to be in Canada?

The usual reasons for emigration. My father was a waiter in Naples. Economically it was a hard existence. Some relatives, my father's brothers, were already in Canada and we joined them. I completed most of my education in Canada. I met Antonio D'Alfonso, whose background is Molisano (actually in Rome in 1984, at the first conference on Italian

Canadian culture). He is the director of Guernica Editions, and publishes primarily Italian Canadian and Italian American authors.

What echoes of Neapolitan cultural life reach North America?

Very few, almost nothing. I collect materials and information when I come to Italy. There is this new journal now that is very useful, *Dove stà Zazà.*

Your nomadic perspective also seems to determine a continuous stylistic experimentation. For example, "The Arsonist" is prose more than poetry.

"The Arsonist" alludes to Dante. It is a piece that refers back to *La vita nuova* and the first canto of the *Commedia.* It is always the search for myself, of a way back. But the fundamental question is "a way back where?" I have no answer.

Crossing Place

An Interview by Rodrigo Toscano

One *of your most recent books of poetry,* The Posthumous
Poet: A Suite for Pier Paolo Pasolini *(Jahbone Press, 1993), not
only invokes the phenomenon that was Pasolini through its title, but the text itself seems intent on mediating Pasolini's
thought (or certain verdicts on Pasolini's thought) through a
condensed and narratively abstracting process that traces the
official events of Pasolini's life as well as the unofficial events
or ideological junctures. In the section entitled "The Enigma of
End," actual titles of Pasolini's works initiate each of the section's pages.*

*What follows might be best described as a critically poetic
encounter by the book's intended author(s). For example, the
first that begins (in bold letters) as "Heretical Empiricism" (Pasolini's 1972) is immediately followed by a gratifyingly fundamental yet difficult pronouncement, "where the poet stands."
The paragraph goes on to work through various time and space
limitations ending with three, more tactically-minded clauses,
"The geography of ideology well defined; the role of the intellectual. Free indirect discourse." Then a typed line suddenly appears across the page splitting it in two. Below it is a one-line
quote from Antonio Gramsci, the one from this piece states,
"Every hegemonic relation is necessarily pedagogic." This ar-
rangement seems to allow a form of critical transparency that
enables the unofficial events/junctures of your ideological existence to be read by way of a poetic map reading. It also seems
reminiscent of some of your previous titles,* Moving Landscape
(1985), A Critical Geography *(1989), and* Nomadic Trajectory *(1990). What might it mean, politically speaking, to be*

writing in this way given that your readership (I'm presuming) is largely comprised of primarily anglophone U.S.A. and Canadian poets or poetry aficionados?

First of all, I'm not really sure that when I started writing *Posthumous Poet* I was thinking of an anglophone reader per se. Also, my association with Italian Canadian poets could probably be taken to refer to that group as a "first reader." But, of course, the anglophone public at large would be the most logical to think of. What might this mean politically speaking? Possibly that I'm placing myself in a position similar to Pasolini's at the time he was writing. His idea of writers' or intellectuals' position was that you could not actually offer a valid interpretation of a person's life-time work until that person was dead because only at that point could one go back and reconstruct, "edit" (in a filmic sense) as he put it — do an edit of a whole person's life and do an interpretation of it. Going back to Pasolini as a way of editing his work to my ends and have them speak in a certain direction which was I believe negated while he was alive. For example, *Lutheran Letters* (1975) is a set of essays in which he very accurately describes the political situation that has in fact come to pass in Italy over the past several months. He made certain accusations concerning leader in the Christian Democrat Party as well as several leaders within the left milieu, that at the time were considered far-fetched, but later turned out to be pretty accurate. This has led some to refer to Pasolini as a prophet, which I think is a ridiculous way of regarding something of the sort. Rather, he was someone who was very much in tune with his time and was able to read certain events in a historical mode, given previous historical occurrences, given certain trends. He was able to, in essence, see how all that worked together. What I am doing now is trying to recuperate his work and by attaching it to Gramsci (a precursor of Pasolini's) extend those into the future. Now, as far as presenting this to an anglophone readership, I guess of the readings that I have done of this book most have been to an anglophone public and to groups who have known Pasolini only sporadically, mostly through one or two films. They might have seen one of his films, might have heard of him, yet haven't read any of his books, don't really know his political/ideological background. I suppose what I'm attempting to do, and what ties into my other books that you mentioned, is a working through language, infiltrating English linguistically through Italian syntax, and particular word usage, for example, the use of latinate words. Some have used that as a point of criticism, without realizing that that's exactly what I'm trying to do, that is to synthesize a language that is not English, that is Italian in English. They've detected this in Italy, for example, Sergio De Santis, writing about me in *La Repubblica* last year, noted that I was an Italian poet writing in English. That's exactly what I've been trying to do all along. In the same way that I'm acting English, I'm also attempting to infiltrate the ideology of that language with someone like Pasolini and someone like Gramsci, because when I read the pieces in *Posthumous Poet* out loud, or when they're read in the book, I don't mention that those are quotes by Gramsci or titles from Pasolini's works. These are in bold type or in quotation marks, or maybe it's quotation M, A, R, X; I'm attempting to infiltrate in that sense. I think it's a pedagogical role that I am aiming for as that quote by Gramsci that you mentioned states. That is why I really emphasize all the time, that I'm not telling stories about my life or someone else's life, I'm not trying to give insights on any particular event. Rather, I'm trying to destabilize those very modes of representation that intend (however unconsciously) to claim the very terrain of political culture on certain bases, the most troubling one for me a hegemonizing bourgeois-individual subjectivity.

Hence, your emphasis on language, your tactic of linguistic/ideological infiltration.

Yes. Though I believe that operation to be to some degree already at work, or that it might be said that the material is somewhat predisposed for such an operation.

You mentioned your identification with some of Paso-lini's problematics, and in turn his identification, or rather in-volvement within Gramsci's problematic; is it a concern for you to disavow any impulse toward tradition, however "unof-ficial" that "tradition" may be?

Generally speaking, yes, it is a concern, but mainly be-cause my interest in Pasolini is not a strict interest. It's an inter-est in trends that are identifiable in Pasolini and that go back to Gramsci. Those equations which I have in *Posthumous Poet* are the points where I think certain connections can be made. The problem with Pasolini that I see is that often he tried to render official — or rather to root — subaltern cultures in what he perceived as a tradition for certain cultures. For in-stance, he was very much attached to the Neapolitan culture, which, to paraphrase him, "had not changed in centuries." Of course it had changed, because of the influence of various groups that had dominated the area for hundreds of years. But any time he perceived a move outside of what he had estab-lished within his own system of beliefs, as what a Southern or Neapolitan norm should be, he was very critical of those moves. Now, I don't subscribe to that at all. I'm not trying to officiate in that sense, because, first of all, as an immigrant to Canada and having looked at the production of Italian immi-grants to Canada as well as the U.S.A., I think we can consider these cultural products and cultural manifestations as part of an Italian continuum. It's not one line, however, but rather one on a multidimensional plane. I've talked about Italian Ca-nadian/Italian American writing as the product of de-contextualized subalterns because it does carry on certain trends that were in motion at the time of emigration, and that were truncated by emigration itself. These then continued out-side in another context and came under the influence of what-ever culture(s) received those immigrants. Then, of course, in Italy the other trunk moved in its different directions there un-der the influence of the Italian nation and so forth — the First and Second World Wars and subsequent interlocking events.

What I am after, what I am interested in looking at and repre-senting (as I do in my writing) is what I said about "infiltrating English with Italian," a hybridization of cultures, which Southern Italian culture, as all cultures are, represents.

Could this multidimensional apprehension of that cul-ture be the cause of the sometimes noted (for lack of a better way to put it) very slight appearance of pronouns in your po-etry?

Very definitely.

Specifically the famous "I" — or maybe even the type of elliptically constructed stanzas . . .

I don't want to blow that up too much but I think — or I'd like to say — that I see myself as part of a collective, how-ever disparate (or desperate) that collective may be. The form of the writing is an attempt, or is a net — is my net that leaves spaces to catch the other voices in the collective. Now, there was one review by someone who said that Pasquale Verdicchio doesn't want to leave the reader any space at all, he wants to lead the reader too strictly by the hand . . . I'm still puzzled at that, because I see that occurring in a more narrative style of poetry, where you are told everything as a reader and are left with little to discover. I believe that I'm working in another di-rection. I'm not however saying that I'm always successful at it.

In retrospect, how do you see Posthumous Poet *fitting (or not fitting) alongside your other works?*

I suppose it fits as an overall trend in various attempts to bridge gaps, gaps in my knowledge, and gaps in the writing that's come before it, and finally gaps in a communication with any imagined reader. Also, I think it's quite different from the other work because it's directed quite openly at one person; Pasolini is the overwhelming presence, the weight which doesn't exist in the other books. Also, since Pasolini was, or became, aware of his contradictions and always went back to critique those contradictions himself, and since I tend to do that in my own work, it set up a unique problematic, one which was new to my poetry.

Can I ask you where Posthumous Poet *was written — what part of the world?*

I spent two weeks at the Pasolini Foundation in Rome, in the summer of 1989, and so parts of it were developed there. The first three pieces were published in *Temblor* (and the book is dedicated to Leland Hickman, the editor of *Temblor* before his death) — those three pieces were written in Rome. The rest were written in San Diego.

Were these pieces conceived as part of a single book?

Yes, that's the way I write — all my books are conceived as books. The only exception might be the last one *Approaches to Absence*, because it also collects *A Critical Geography* (a chapbook from 1990) and "Translatio," which appeared in the journal *The Raddle Moon*.

"Translatio," as in "to carry across . . ."?

Right.

*Though you might ascertain that as far as this "carrying across," that some things are indeed not carried but are left (is it behind?). I'm thinking of the blurb that you've written for Ap-*proaches to Absence, *a sort of shorthand definition of culture.*

Well, here it is, I'll read it: "Home is established by our relationship to the world around us, wherever we are. Nevertheless, we also occupy the places of our absence. Culture is constructed, in passing through a place, in what is taken through the departure, in what is left behind. Culture is a matter of subtraction and offering." This contains various aspects of what I intend as culture. A matter of subtraction and offering, the materiality of culture, first of all, and that (again) touches on what we said about Pasolini earlier: in not attempting to root Southern Culture / my culture / immigrant culture. I don't think any culture anywhere can strictly be spoken of as rooted. Yes, I think the subtractive aspect of culture is just as important; that deracination/emigration means something about the nature of a particular culture.

So much of history in general has been uprooting, espe-
cially in this century — and even more recently, we seem to be
living within a new surge of uprooting. In some ways, I see
your work as a sort of ethos or even pathos of displacement.
You seem to want to (however eagerly or reluctantly) to inhabit
that . . . a kind of "crossing-place" — but that's your bind — is
that, that is what we inhabit, hence Nomadic Trajectory.

Yes, "nomadic trajectory," and that that's the oases, the
places in between, between where we're going and where
we've come form. Again, we're uprooted because of certain
historical uprooting.

So that by de-mystifying this thing of "origin," doesn't
that leave the reader or yourself ready for a different kind of po-
litical awareness that acknowledges the pseudo-histories of ori-
gin and nationalism?

Hopefully, but it's not just a matter of acknowledgment,
but ideological convergence.

In a manner of not adhering to Pasolini's observations on
the question of the periodization of a writer's work before his or
her death. I remember your once commenting that your genera-
tion (mainly within Italy) has been spoken of as a "lost genera-
tion," following certain political defeats in and around 1968.
So could it be said that that generation is not only interested in
things that collapse but also is interested in being able to deal
with things collapsing, even as a sort of ground.

I tend to think so. Though to a large degree this is due to
the inherent contradictions within movements, cultures and
the like. I'm used to things collapsing. I suppose I might even
say I live that. I sometimes have a hard time dealing with
groups because as soon as the cracks in my perception of the
group start to show up I think it's time for me to move on.

How do you prevent (if this a concern for you) from that
becoming a suggestive prescription for a mere "personal" type
of praxis? Or is it a strategy employed to retain both the speci-
ficity and generality of your political/cultural existence; maybe

one (among many) of possible constitutions of a kind of "mass-individual."

Maybe a mass-individual, coalitions that are elastic, ones that can be made more transparent, to remain mobile enough to resist their static elements and the dogmatism of ideology.

Notes

Subalterns Abroad

1. While I intend to stress that Southern Italian emigration was the result of colonial policies and activities on the part of the expanding House of Piedmont, I would also emphasize that the repression of cultural diversity manifested itself in areas outside of the South, especially in poorer regions such as the Friuli.

2. Interesting reading in this regard may include Arthur M. Schlesinger Jr.'s *The Disuniting of America: Reflections on a Multicultural Society* (New York: Norton, 1992).

3. Of course, a most interesting relationship is also established between each new-comer group and others struggling for status. The African American community appears to have been the target of most immigrant groups' calumnies in the latter's struggle to assimilate. I analyze the relationships between Italian Americans and African Americans in Spike Lee's films in "If I was six feet tall I would have been Italian."

4. ". . . Benedetto Croce has fulfilled an extremely important 'national' function, by having detached the radical intellectuals of the South from the peasant masses and having them partecipate in national and European culture; and through this culture, he has caused their absorption by the national bourgeoisie and hence by the agrarian bloc" (Antonio Gramsci, *The Southern Question,* translated by Pasquale Verdicchio (Chicago: Bordighera, 1995).

5. Gramsci, ibid.

6. Antonio Gramsci, *La questione meridionale* (Roma: Editori Riuniti, 1966), and *Gli intellettuali* (Roma: Editori Riuniti, 1977). The latter is a collection of materials collated from Gramsci's *Quaderni del carcere* (Prison Notebooks). The geographic designation of "the South and the Islands" defines the empoverished areas of Italy. This large region encompasses approximately half of the Italian landmass. The effects of the "economic boom" of the postwar era largely left it behind; industrialization has almost consistently failed, and the stereotypic imaging of Southerners as a primitive and uncultured

sector of Italy still subsists in racist expressions such as "Africa begins at Naples."

7. Historical inactivity does not mean cultural inactivity; however, cultural activity itself may in fact produce historically active factors that may go un-noticed or unrecognized until a later period.

8. Antonio Gramsci, *Prison Notebooks*, edited and translated by Quintin Hoare and Geoffrey N. Smith, ninth printing (New York: International Publishers, 1987), 360. In Gramscian terms POSSIBILITY=FREEDOM. Even a superficially open environment like the Canadian "multicultural mosaic" provides enough of a possibility for groups to take up a struggle for self representation.

9. Within the Gramscian differentiation of the concept of hegemony, "hegemonic principle" is that by which the official culture takes into account the demands of a certain group only to neutralize it and prevent its extention. "Expansive hegemony" is the process by which equivalences between groups are found that support the demands of equality of a number of groups.

10. A notable recent example of the vast divisions that still hinder a full expression of Italian cultural diversity is Giorgio Bocca's *La disUnità d'Italia: Per venti milioni di italiani la democrazia è in coma e l'Europa s'allontana* (Milano: Garzanti, 1990).

11. The reference here is to English as the target language. This relationship is also evident in many Italian Canadian writers from Quebec who write in (or also in) French. Of particular importance here are Fulvio Caccia's *Irpinia* (Montreal: Triptyque/Guernica, 1983) and *Scirocco* (Montreal: Triptyque, 1985), and Antonio D'Alfonso's novel *Avril ou l'anti-passion* (Montreal: Vlb éditeur, 1990). I wish to point out that *The Other Shore* was also published in French as *L'autre rivage* (Montreal: VLB éditeur, 1986).

12. I use aggregate because it maintains a sense of individuality within the grouping, rather than propose an individual vs. group paradigm.

13. I believe that a transformation such as the one alluded to by McLuhan is also definable in terms of the metamorphosis from emigrant to immigrant. The "moment of change" is also a potential moment of challenge in which the individual or group may elect to challenge both the culture from which s/he emigrated and the one into which s/he immigrated.

14. Published in the journal, *ViceVersa*, No. 26. *ViceVersa* is a multilingual publication out of Montreal, whose initial founders included Antonio D'Alfonso, Fulvio Caccia, and Lamberto Tassinari.

15. "Pasquale *(to Jacques, quickly showing his pride)*: See how he speaks English. He doesn't let on. But . . . He speaks English like the English and French better than the French. I know, because I understand him, but not a word of the French in this place. *(Then, as if revealing a secret)*. Only Italian, he doesn't speak it very well. *(In the normal tone again.)* He, then, the poor boy, already has nothing to say. Then he had the misfortune to end up with us. *(Louder in excellent Italian.)* We have even forgotten Italian. *(He continues in dialect.)* What's money, houses, cars and everything else, if we've lost the most beautiful thing there is. There is nothing more beautiful. We don't know how to talk anymore. *(With contained anger.)* At times, I'd sell everything and leave . . . *(Turning toward the audience.)* How do you feel, when your children speak to you in English or French knowing fully well that you only understand Molisian or Abrutian."
Molisian and Abrutian are dialect variations of the Abruzzi-Molise region.

16. Just a reminder here that Showstack-Sassoon offers a similar position in relation to hegemony.

17. Paulo Freire, *Cultural Action for Freedom*, Harvard Educational Review, Monograph, Series No. 1 (Cambridge: Harvard Educational Review, 1988). *Conscientization* is a term used by the Brazilian intellectual Paulo Freire to refer to a population's "critical self-insertion into reality," or as expressed by the editor of the English translation: "the process in which men, not as recipients, but as knowing subjects, achieve a deepening awareness both of the socio-cultural reality which shapes their lives and of their capacity to transform that reality."

18. Traditional intellectuals have their own "organic" group. However, the distinction is to be made between those who remain in the service of their group (organic) and those who serve the interests of the dominant or traditional (read also national) culture against those of their own.

The Borders of Writing

1. An effort was made to recognize Villa's importance with the publication of the special issue of *Uomini e idee* (Anno xviii, n. 2-4, ottobre 1975) dedicated to Emilio Villa, an initiative taken mostly through the influence of the poets Adriano Spatola and Luciano Caruso. I am indebted to that issue for much of my own knowledge of Emilio Villa. His first published work is *Adolescenza* (Bologna, 1934), a rather traditional collection which was followed by many limited edition publications such as *Oramai* (Roma, 1947), *Villadrome* (Roma, 1964), *Traitée de pédérasthie céleste* (Napoli, 1969), and *Le mûra di t;éb;é* (Brescia, 1981).

Tracing the Ground of Identity

1. See "The Preclusion of Postcolonial Discourse in Southern Italy," in *Designing Italy,* Beverly Allen and Mary Russo, editors. (Minneapolis: University of Minnesota Press, 1997).
2. Whether due to reasons of external construction, or for other questions of self-identity, Southern Italians themselves are, to some extent, black-identified. This is of course a result of the Mediterranean, rather than European, sphere of influence in which the Italian South has moved throughout time. Pino Daniele and James Senese's music, as on the albums *Nero a metà* and *Anema nera* respectively, are but two contemporary examples of this affiliation. As of late, raggamuffin groups have further extended the reach to Africa in their music. The title of the Neapolitan group Alma Megretta's recent release, "Sons of Hannibal," speaks for itself. These representations of mestisization are blended into other figures steeped in traditional popular culture such as Pulcinella, who is often extended into a characterization of the mythical/popular revolutionary figure of Masaniello. Another important figure in Southern culture is Gennariello, quintessential representation of Neapolitan culture in the films of Elvira Notari (Giuliana Bruno, *Streetwalking on a Ruined Map,* 1993) during the 1920s, whose physiognomy is most definitely African. Whether knowingly or not, in his "A Little Pedagogical Treatise" (1975), Pier Paolo Pasolini instrumentalized the name Gennariello to construct a particu-

larly strong representation of a young Neapolitan boy as the figure of the Other in Italian society.

3. See "If I was six feet tall I would have been Italian: Spike Lee's Guineas" in this collection.

4. Such representations are common in Literature, Imperialist Rhetoric, and Political commentary. Another citation worth recording from A. Niceforo's *Contemporary Barbarian Italy* (1898) is as follows: "No other people of Italy are as light, fickle, and restless like the Neapolitans; a lightness that is truly womanly . . . The Neapolitans are, in contrast to the manly populations, such as northern Italians, Germans, and English, a womanly population" (in Teti, 247-248). The following are two studies that offer a wide range of readings of the feminization of geographic/colonized space: "Love Songs from the Tomb: Female Voice in Foscolo's 'Dei sepolcri,' Margaret Brose, UC Santa Cruz, unpublished manuscript; *Nationalism and Sexualities,* edited by Andrew Parker, Mary Russo, Doris Sommer, and Patricia Yaeger (N.Y.: Routledge, 1992).

5. Throughout the pages of a special issue of *sinister wisdom,* no. 41, on Italian American Women, it is also obvious that the question of racial identity is of extreme importance to Southern Italian women.

6. Though I have used Charles Taylor's term "politics of recognition,"I want to distance myself from his pro-Quebecois stance which, through the oppression and erasure of other cultures within Quebec in order to maintain its officiality, contradicts its stated purpose.

More than a Thematic Approach

1. See "Reflecting Today's Ethnic Reality" by C.D. Minni in *Writers in Transition.*

A Non Canon

1. As emigrant writers, we have Vittorini's beautiful illustration of this in his *Conversazione in Sicilia.* Elio Vittorini, *Conversazione in Sicilia* (Torino: Einaudi, 1978), 14. The traveller, a Sicilian who has been living in the north of Italy and is returning to his native land, finds himself confronted with a question of identity, which he resolves linguistically: "Soggiunse:

— Siete americano voi? Parlava con disperazione eppure con
soavità, come sempre era stato soave anche nel disperato pe-
lare l'arancia e nel disperato mangiarla. Le ultime tre parole
disse eccitato, in tono di stridula tensione come se gli fosse in
qualche modo necessario, per la pace dell'anima, sapermi
americano. — Sì, — dissi io, vedendo questo. — Americano
sono. Da quindici anni.

2. Jean Braudillard, " . . . Or the end of the social," in *In the
    Shadow of the Silent Majorities and Other Essays* (New York:
    Semiotext, 1983), 70.

Bibliography

Allen, Beverly and Mary Russo, eds. *Designing Italy*. Minneapolis: University of Minnesota Press, 1996.

Arrighi, Giovanni, Terence K. Hopkins and Immanurl Wallerstein. *Antisystemic Movements*. New York: Verso, 1989.

Artaud, Antonin. *Oeuvres complètes*. Vol. 9. Paris: Gallimard, 1971.

Azpadu, Dodici. *Saturday Night in the Prime of Life*. Iowa City: Aunt Lute, 1983.

Bocca, Giorgio. *La disUnità d'Italia: Per venti milioni di italiani la democrazia è in coma e l'Europa s'allontana*. Milano: Garzanti, 1990.

Bona, Mary Jo, ed. *The Voices We Carry*. Montreal: Guernica, 1994.

Braudillard, Jean. ". . . Or the end of the social." In *In the Shadow of the Silent Majorities and Other Essays*. New York, Semiotext, 1983.

Bucci Bush, Mary. *Drowning*. San Diego: Parentheses, 1995.

Caccia, Fulvio. *Irpinia*. Montreal: Tryptique/Guernica, 1983.

—————. *Scirocco*. Montreal: Tryptique, 1985.

—————. *Aknos*. Toronto: Guernica, 1994.

Clifford, James and George E. Marcus, eds. *Writing Culture: The Poetics and Politics of Ethnography*. Berkeley: UC Press, 1986.

D'Alfonso, Antonio. *The Other Shore*. Montreal: Guernica, 1986.

—————. *Avril ou l'anti-passion*. Montreal: Vlb éditeur, 1990.

—————. *Fabrizio's Passion*. Toronto: Guernica, 1995.

—————. *In Italics: In Defense of Ethnicity*. Toronto: Guernica, 1996.

Davis, F. James. *Who is Black? One Nation's Definition*. University Park: Penn State University Press, 1991.

Deleuze, Gilles and Felix Guattari. *Kafka: Toward a Minor Literature*. Minneapolis: Univesity of Minnesota, 1986.

Derrida, Jacques. *Writing and Difference*. Chicago: University of Chicago, 1978.

—————. "Signature, Event, Content." In *Glyph 1*. Baltimore: John Hopkins Textual Studies, 1977.

Di Cicco, Pier Giorgio, ed. *Roman Candles: An Anthology of 17 Italo-Canadian Poets.* Toronto: Anansi, 1978.

Edwards, Caterina. *A Whiter Shade of Pale.* (Edmonton: NeWest, 1992).

——————. *The Lion's Mouth.* Toronto: Guernica, 1994.

Fante, John. *Ask the Dust.* Santa Barbara, Black Sparrow, 1980.

Ferrini, Vincent. *Know Fish.* Storrs: University of Connecticut Library, 1979.

Freire, Paulo. *Cultural Action for Freedom.* Monograph Series No 1. Cambridge: Harvard Educational Review, 1988.

Gramsci, Antonio. *La questione meridionale.* Roma: Editori Riuniti, 1966.

——————. *Gli intellettuali.* Roma: Editori Riuniti, 1977.

——————. Selections for the *Prison Notebooks.* Edited and translated by Quintin Hoare and Geoffrey N. Smith. Ninth Printing. New York: International Publishers, 1987.

——————. *The Southern Question.* Translated, annotated and introduced by Pasquale Verdicchio. Chicago: Bordighera, 1995.

Grizzutti Harrison, Barbara. "Spike Lee Hates Your Cracker Ass." In *Esquire,* October 1992, 132-140.

Harlow, Barbara. *Resistance Literature.* 1987.

Jenkins, Henry and Mary Fuller. "Nintendo's Super Mario Bros." In *Civitas,* Fall 93: 1-8.

Laclau, Ernesto and Chantall Mouffe. *Hegemony and Socialist Strategy.* London: Verso, 1986.

Larsen, Susan. C. "Italo Scanga: Confronting the Spirits." In *ARTnews,* November 1984.

Lecercle, Jean-Jacques. *Philosophy Through the Looking Glass.* La Salle: Open Court, 1985.

Lee, Spike and Lisa Jones. *Do the Right Thing.* New York: Fireside, 1989.

Loriggio, Francesco. *Social Pluralism and Literary History: The Literature of Italian Immigration.* Toronto: Guernica, 1996.

Maso, Carol. *Ava.* Normal: Dalkey Archive, 1993.

McLuhan, Marshall. *Through the Vanishing Point: Space in Poetry and Painting.* New York: Harper & Row, 1968.

Melfi, Mary. *Infertility Rites.* Montreal: Guernica, 1991.

Michelut, Dôre. *Loyalty to the Hunt.* Montreal: Guernica, 1986.

Micone, Marco. *Gens du silence.* Monteal: Guernica, 1982.

——————————. *Voiceless People*. Translated by Maurizia Binda. Montreal: Guernica, 1984.

Minni, Dino and Anna Foschi Ciampolini. *Writers in Transition: The Proceedings of the First National Conference of Italian-Canadian Writers*. Montreal: Guernica, 1990.

Mouffe, Chantall. "For a politics of nomadic identity." In *Travellers' Tales. Narrative of Home and Displacement*. Robertson et al., eds. New York: Routledge, 1994.

——————————. "Hegemony and New Political Subjects: Toward a New Concept of Democracy." In *Marxism and the Interpretation of Culture*. C. Nelson and L. Grossberg, eds. Chicago: University of Illinois Press, 1988.

Musser, Charles. "Ethnicity, Role-Playing, and American Film Comedy. From Chinese Laundry Scene to Whoopee (1894-1930)." In *Unspeakable Images: Ethnicity and the American Cinema*, L. Friedman ed. Chicago: University of Illinois, Press, 1991.

Paglia, Camille. *Sex, Art, and American Culture*. New York: Vintage, 1992.

Perin, Roberto and Frank Sturino, eds. *Arrangiarsi: The Italian Immigration Experience in Canada*. Montreal: Guernica, 1989.

Pivato, Joseph. *Contrasts*. Montreal: Guernica 1986.

Reid, Mark A. *Redefining Black Film*. Berkeley: UC Press, 1993.

Romano, Rose. *The Wop Factor*. Brooklyn: malafemmina press, 1994.

Showstack Sassoon, Anne. *Gramsci's Politics*. New York: St. Martin's Press, 1980.

Schlesinger, Arthur M. Jr. *The Disuniting of America: Reflections on a Multicultural Society*. New York: Norton, 1992.

Sorrentino, Gilbert. *Aberration of Starlight*. New York: Penguin, 1980.

——————————. *Blue Pastoral*. San Francisco: North Point Press, 1983.

——————————. *Something Said*. San Francisco: North Point Press, 1984.

Tamburri, Anthony Julian, Paolo Giordano and Fred Gardaphé, eds. *From the Margins: Writings in Italian Americana*. West Lafayette: Purdue University Press, 1991.

Villa, Emilio. *Opere poetiche I*. Edited and introduced by Aldo Tagliaferri. Milano: Coliseum, 1989.

——————. *Seventeen Variations on Proposed Themes for a Pure Phonetic Ideology.* Translated by Pasquale Verdicchio. Limited edition. San Diego: Parentheses, 1990.

Wolfson, Louis. *Le Schizo et les langages.* Paris: Gallimard, 1970.

Zanzotto, Andrea. *Fosfeni.* Milano: Mondadori, 1983.

Acknowledgments

"Subalterns Abroad" previously appeared in *Social Pluralism and Literary History,* edited by Francesco Loriggio (Guernica, 1996). "The Borders of Writing" was presented at the Philosophy and Literature Conference of the International Philosophical Association in Edmonton, Alberta, 1994. "Tracing the Ground of Identity" was presented at the Association of Italian Canadian Writers Conference in Winnipeg, Manitoba, 1994. "Fante's Inferno" was presented at the First Fante Conference, Cal State Long Beach, California, 1995. "There Dago!" was presented at the Chicago Conference of the American Italian Historical Association, 1994. "If I was six feet tall . . ." previously appeared in *Differentia* 6/7, 1996. "The Intellectual Ghetto," "The Failure of Memory," and "A Non Canon" were presented at the first Association of Italian Canadian conference in Vancouver, B.C., 1986, and later published in *Writers in Transition,* edited by Dino Minni and Anna Foschi Ciampolino (Guernica, 1990). "Writing Out of Tonue" was presented at Small Press Distribution, Berkeley, Ca. 1988. "Italo Scanga's *A Troubled World*" appeared in *Artspace.* "Tina Modotti" was presented at the International Modotti Conference, University of California, San Diego, 1996. "A Poet in a Moving Landscape" appeared in *Vice Versa,* No. 16, 1986. "Scattered Verses Between Naples and Canada" appeared in *La Repubblica,* Nov 12, 1993. "Crossing Place" appeared in *The Washington Review,* June 1994. Sections of "Subalterns Abroad," "Tracing the Ground of Identity," and "If I were six feet tall . . ." have beed incorporated in the book *Bound by Distance: Rethinking Nationalism through the Italian Diaspora* (Farleigh Dickinson, 1997).

By the Same Author

Moving Landscape (1985)
Ipsissima verba (1986)
A Critical Geography (1990)
Nomadic Trajectory (1990)
Isthmus (1991)
The Posthumous Poet:
A Suite for Pier Paolo Pasolini (1993)
Approaches to Absence (1994)

AGMV
MARQUIS
Québec, Canada
1997

DATE DUE

JUN 0 2 1999		
JUN 1 0 1999		
DEC 2 2 1999		
DEC 1 3 1999		

Demco, Inc. 38-293